CHURCH PRINCIPLES FOR TODAY

Transcribed from lectures given by
Rowan Jennings

© 1997 Thomas Jennings.

First published in Great Britian in 1997

All rights reserved.

No part of this publication may be reproduced or transmitted, in any form or by any means, electronic or mechanical, including photocopying, recording, or any information storage and retrieval system, without permission in writing.

Published, Designed and Printed by:

Bible Studies Institute,

Lower Glenageary Road, Dun Laoghaire, Co. Dublin, Ireland.

I dedicate this book to Mr. & Mrs. Norman Emerson (Ardmore), Mrs. Campbell and Sammy (Annalong) and all those dear saints, at home and abroad, who ministered and encouraged my father in his many years of service to his Lord.

Table of Contents

Rightly Dividing the Word of Truth	11
The Church and the Churches	45
The Baptism in the Spirit	109
The Gifts of the Spirit	147
Baptism	181
The Lord's Supper	217
Assembly Discipline	253
Headship	291
The Grace Of Giving	315
Appendix	340
Index	343

FOREWORD

I counted it a real privilege to have known the late Rowan Jennilngs personally for many years. In his early days he was in fellowship in the same assembly as my wife, I met him while visiting there in the early 1950's. It was evident then, that he was a person who has a real thirst for the deep things of God. The constant reading and study of the Word of God soon produced one who had studied to shew himself "approved unto God, a workman that needeth not to be ashamed, rightly dividing the word of truth (2 Tim 2:15). Some of the lasting fruit of such study has already been made available in his previous book, "Future Events", which has been extremely well received

This volume is dedicated to the consideration of New Testament church principles, which Mr. Jennings held dear and taught well to the people of God in many places. Apart from dealing with various assembly subjects, the book commences with a very helpful outline of the arrangement of the books of the New Testament followed by important aspects of the structure of those books which came from the pen of the apostle Paul. Careful reading of this chapter will give great help to all who are prepared to read it. Our brother believed, and supports it well, that the actual arrangement of the NT books is by no means haphazard, rather that God carefully guided the very order of the books as they are found. This is the more interesting when we see that they were not historically written in such order. A perusal of the chapter headings will show many vital subjects which all who are in assembly fellowship need to understand.

The style of this book is not formal, the unique way in which our late brother presented truth has been retained so that those who heard him will be reminded of his ministry as they read. It would be difficult to find any book which earns total approval for every view expounded, yet here there is much to profit and educate the enquiring mind. It certainly is an exposition of "those things which are most surely believed among us" (Luke 1:1). May our beloved Lord bless its ministry to the generation of our day.

J.R.Baker
March, 1997.

PREFACE

In 1993, as a result of the encouragement of God's people, to put into print some of the teaching of my late father, Mr. Rowan Jennings, Belfast, I commenced work on the book, "Future Events". This book was first published, in 1994, and had to go into reprint in the same year.

As a result of this encouragement and the continued promptings of the saints, I have now undertaken this second work.

Some will argue that such subjects, as those dealt with in, "Church Principles for Today", are so widely known that their teaching is unnecessary; however, others might equally argue, that they are not taught enough and are seen as tradition and should, therefore, be set aside. I, however, feel that I can answer both arguments, when I recall that Paul the Apostle stated, in Philippians, chapter 3, verse 1, that the repetition of Truth will lead to the safety of the saints, and this he confirms, in II Timothy, chapter 2, verse 14, as also does the Apostle Peter, in II Peter, chapter 1, verse 12. This book has, therefore, been written in order to remind the saints of these precious Truths, so dearly held by us.

Further, as I travel amongst God's people, not only in Northern Ireland, but across Europe, I notice that a recurrent theme of conversation is the apparent sad spiritual condition of many Christians. While it would be unwise to point the finger at the stated reasons, we must all confess that two of the main arguments must be the lack of suitable consecutive teaching and our own lack of endeavour in delving into the beauties of God's revealed mind and will, for us. We recall, from Luke, chapter 24, that the Lord Jesus, on resurrection ground, taught the two disciples on the way to Emmaus, the things concerning Himself, from the Old Testament Scriptures. We are told, that their very hearts "burned" within them, from the sheer joy from that to which they were listening. This book is aimed to the renewing of that joy, and hunger, for the things of God.

However, some might argue that such a book is simply unsuitable for today! Our young people react to the teaching of doctrine as tradition, while others, of its verging on exclusiveism. What I have sought to do is to show that there is one overriding aim as to why the Lord introduced these various doctrines and practices for His Churches and that was to emphasise His Lordship, in the lives of His People.

The types of people I have had in mind, as I progressed through this work, were many: Firstly, I would be hoping that young saints will benefit from the clarity of the Biblical arguments set forth for some of our traditions and practices; secondly, I would trust that the shepherds, of our Churches, would be encouraged to uphold these same doctrines, in a righteous and even manner, as they guide us towards the Judgement Seat of Christ; and finally, that those young men, aspiring to taking a leading role, will consider the responsibility, as well as the honour, of those leading positions.

Finally, I wish to sincerely thank all those who assisted me in this endeavour without whose encouragement the work would not have progressed. Firstly, Eric and Glo Davis, Dublin, who worked so hard in publishing the book, Miss Penny DeFouw, who transcribed the origional tapes, Mr. Joe Skelly, who permitted his recordings to be used and Drs. William and Samuel-

James McBride and Mr. Noel Davidson, who proof read the script.

I commend this work to the Lord and to His grace.

Thomas Jennings.
Belfast, 1997.

Chapter 1

Rightly Dividing the Word of Truth

The subjects we are about to deal with, in this book, are of a different kind to those generally studied. They are directed to those who have an interest in the Scriptures, in general, and in Church Principles, in particular, so that we might all begin to understand the mind and will of God a little better, as regards His wishes for our Church practices.

Our first subject, "Rightly dividing the Word of Truth", will give us, what I consider, to be the way to study our Bible, so that we will then be able to comprehend God's plans as revealed in His Word and so be in a position to put them into practice.

The passage we are going to study, in this first chapter, is the:

Epistle of the Romans, chapter 8, verses 33 to 39:

"Who shall lay any thing to the charge of God's elect? It is God that justifieth. Who is He that condemneth? It is Christ that died, yea rather, that is risen again, who is even at the right hand of God, who also maketh intercession for us. Who shall separate us from the love of Christ? Shall tribulation, or distress, or persecution, or famine, or nakedness, or peril, or sword? As it is written, For thy sake we are killed all the day long; we are accounted as sheep for the slaughter. Nay, in all these things we are more than conquerors through Him that loved us. For I am persuaded, that neither death, nor life, nor angels, nor principalities, nor powers, nor things present, nor things to come, nor height, nor depth, nor any other creature, shall be able to separate us from the love of God, which is in Christ Jesus our Lord."

Then a verse in chapter 11, verse 33:

Rightly Dividing the Word of Truth

"O the depth of the riches both of the wisdom and knowledge of God! How unsearchable are his judgments, and his ways past finding out! For who hath known the mind of the Lord? Or who hath been his counsellor? Or who hath first given to him, and it shall be recompensed unto him again. For of him, and through him, and to him, are all things: to whom be glory for ever. Amen."

Introduction to Paul's Life

I am sure that most of us are well aware of the fact that Paul the Apostle made a number of missionary journeys.

Figure 1.1:   **Paul's First Missionary Journey**

Church Principles for Today

The first journey he made we could call, "Missionary Journey Number 1". You can read the whole story of that short journey in the Acts of the Apostles, chapter 13. See Figure 1.1. Quite a number of things happened during that journey which I am not going to explain, but that was his first.

After a while he made, "Missionary Journey Number 2". We read about that also in the Acts of the Apostles. That journey was a longer one. He passed over into Macedonia, where he visited Corinth, Philippi, Athens, and so on, and after a fairly extended visit, he went home. See Figure 1.2.

Figure 1.2:   Paul's Second Missionary Journey

Then, after a little while, he made "Missionary Journey Number 3". On that journey, he retraced the steps of his second journey. So again, he was in Macedonia, again, he was in Greece and, again, after a fairly extended journey, he went home. See Figure 1.3.

Figure 1.3: **Paul's Third Missionary Journey**

After this he was apprehended and brought to Rome (see Figure 1.4) and there he was put in prison. I am going to call that, "Imprisonment Number 1". That imprisonment takes us to the end of the Acts of the Apostles, where the last verse, but one, of chapter

Church Principles for Today

28, speaks about his being confined to a hired house - in a word - in jail.

So, if you were to carefully study the Acts of the Apostles, from chapter 13, you would be brought right through his first missionary journey, through his second, through his third and into his first imprisonment.

Now, I think that I could satisfactorily prove to anyone, who is interested, that Paul was released from that particular imprisonment and made a fourth missionary journey. So, "Missionary Journey Number 4". But that fourth journey will not be

Figure 1.4:   **Paul's First Imprisonment**

Rightly Dividing the Word of Truth

found in the Acts of the Apostles at all, you need not look for it, for it is not there. However, if we were to study the rest of the New Testament, we would soon come to the conclusion that Paul was released from that imprisonment and made that fourth and final missionary journey.

Then, he was apprehended a second time and, again, was put in prison in Rome. So, "Imprisonment Number 2", and it was during this second imprisonment that he was slain.

So Paul's life is very, very plain and beautiful to study. See Table 1.1.

Missionary Journey Number 1	- Acts of the Apostles, chapter 13:2-14:27
Missionary Journey Number 2	- Acts of the Apostles, chapter 15:36-18:22
Missionary Journey Number 3	- Acts of the Apostles, chapter 18:23-21:17
Imprisonment Number 1	- Acts of the Apostles, chapter 26:31-28:16
Missionary Journey Number 4	
Imprisonment Number 2	

Table 1.1: Paul's Ministry

Paul's Writings

Would it not be a lovely thing, to try to find out what books Paul wrote and where he was when he wrote them?

Indeed, if you were to make a careful study of this very thing you would find that in his first missionary journey he did not write any books at all. As shown above, that journey was not very long. (There was a little bit of trouble in it, when, in chapter 13, verse 13, John Mark, who had accompanied Paul and Barnabas, returned home). However, during the second missionary journey he wrote two books: I and II Thessalonians. Then, on his third missionary journey, he wrote four more books: I and II Corinthians, Galatians and Romans. After that he was put in jail.

During the time of this first imprisonment he wrote a further four books: The first one he wrote was Ephesians, then he wrote Philippians, then he wrote the little book called Philemon and, finally, he wrote the Epistle to the Colossians.

Now these first-imprisonment-books are all short, so it would not take very long to read them. If you were to read the Ephesian Epistle, look for "my bonds" (chapter, 6:20) and "my imprisonment" (chapters, 3:1; 4:1). He is talking about, "my bonds", because he is in prison. He does not say that in I or II Thessalonians, nor in I or II Corinthians, nor in Galatians, nor in Romans, because he was not in jail when he wrote those. But

Rightly Dividing the Word of Truth

he certainly was in jail when he wrote to the Ephesians. Read it and see!

When you come to the Epistle to the Philippians, look for "salvation" (chapter, 1:19) and look out for "bonds" (chapter, 1:7, 13, 14, 16). They are everywhere. So the Epistle to the Philippians was written in jail also.

If you were to read the little Epistle to Philemon, then look for "bonds" (verses 10, 13), "imprisonment" (verse 1) and "fellow prisoners" (verse 23). Again, he was in jail. Then, when you read the Epistle to the Colossians, look for "sufferings" (chapter, 1:24), "chains" (chapter, 4:3, 18), "fellow prisoners" (chapter, 4:10) and so on, because when he wrote to the Colossians he was in jail.

(Now, that should help you to understand those books. It should give you an insight into each book that ordinarily you would not have. If you were to study the Philippian Epistle, without reference to these things, you would not understand it in the same light. This background knowledge helps you to understand it.)

Church Principles for Today

During his fourth missionary journey, Paul wrote yet another two books: I Timothy and the little book, called Titus. You will find, if you read both of those books, that he speaks about things that could not possibly be fitted into the Acts of the Apostles. We come to the conclusion, therefore, that he must have been released from prison and during a fourth missionary journey he wrote I Timothy and Titus.

When he writes I Timothy, he says, 'O that I might finish my course', because at this stage he knows that his death is not far off. But, there is one thing he does not want to happen: He does not want to go Home until his course is finished.

Not long after that he is apprehended a second time and during that final imprisonment he wrote II Timothy. But this time he says, "... I am now ready to be offered, and the time of my departure is at hand. I have fought a good fight, I have finished my course, I have kept the faith..." (chapter, 4:6, 7).

(When I read those words, I long to be like him. I often pray that prayer of Paul's, as in I Timothy, 'O that I might finish my course'. I long to have the realisation, in my soul, that someday I will have finished my course, when the time of my own departure is at hand.)

So when we look at these things, we find the order in which the books of the New Testament were written. This is sometimes called, 'The Chronological Order of the Writing of Paul's Books'. See Table 1.2.

Missionary Journey Number 1	- No books written.
Missionary Journey Number 2	- I & II Thessalonians.
Missionary Journey Number 3 and Romans.	- I & II Corinthians, Galatians
Imprisonment Number 1	- Ephesians, Philippians, Colossians and Philemon.
Missionary Journey Number 4	- I Timothy and Titus.
Imprisonment Number 2	- II Timothy.

Table 1.2: The Chronological Order of Paul's Writings

The Order of New Testament Books

Of all the epistles of Paul, there are four that are most beautiful: That little book of Titus, that little book of Philemon and those letters of I and II Timothy. These four books are called,

Church Principles for Today

'The Pastoral Epistles', and they are all placed together in your New Testament.

Do you know why they are placed together? Because they were written by a pastor, to pastors; they were written by an overseer, to overseers; they were written by a bishop, to bishops; they were written by a shepherd, to shepherds; they were written by an elder, to elders. So that if anybody, at anytime, would like to find some information about a pastor, an overseer, a bishop, a shepherd or an elder, then he only has to go to I and II Timothy, Titus and Philemon and he will find the whole story. God, in His grace, has taken those four books and put themtogether in your Bible.

(I was delighted at an Easter conference meeting, in Belfast, many years ago when, for the first time in all my life, I heard a man declare, from the public platform, that he believed that the order of the books in our Bible was divinely arranged. I did not say anything to him about it, but I went home all glad. Indeed, I was absolutely delighted.)

If we would count what was left of Paul's epistles we would find that we have nine: One of those is a set of I and II Thessalo-

Rightly Dividing the Word of Truth

nians; the other is a set of I and II Corinthians. If we were to take those together as one book each, then we have seven epistles by Paul. (It is an interesting fact that there are seven letters to the Churches of Asia, in Revelation, chapters 2 and 3. Perhaps there is a connection!) We do well to call these epistles, 'The Church Epistles'. Again, they are all together and, of course, absolutely distinct from those books which start from the Epistle to the Hebrews and go through to the Book of the Revelation. Those have an entirely different context, which must also be understood. See Figure 1.5.

Now, what I want to do for a little while is to take those let-

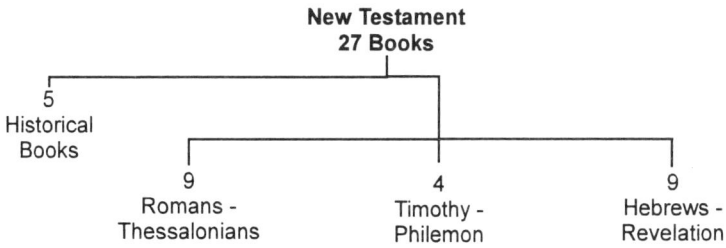

Figure 1:5   **The Balance of the New Testament Writings**

ters of Paul and see what they are all about.

The first one we find in our New Testament, however, is not

Church Principles for Today

the Thessalonians, which is what Paul wrote first. God puts that last! The first one God uses is the Epistle to the Romans. Then we find two books: Corinthians and Galatians. After that you have that beautiful book, called Ephesians, and then two little books, Philippians and Colossians. Finally, you have Thessalonians. See Figure 1.6

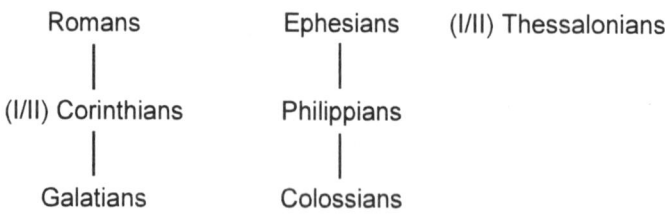

Figure 1.6: **The Order of Paul's Writings**

Now that order is vital. If you can understand these simple things that I am trying to put before you, you will be able to read these books in an intelligent way and be able to see how they all fit together. Also, when you see this overall plan, you will understand the contents much better.

For years, I have taught that if you want to read a book in either the Old Testament or the New Testament, the first thing you should do is find its structure. That may be difficult to do but you should do it nevertheless. You must find out what the

Rightly Dividing the Word of Truth

book is about; you have to find its thrust; you have to find its overall meaning; you have to find out how the book is put together. Once you have found that, the meaning of the individual passages fit in without any difficulty at all.

For example, if you would read the Epistle to the Romans you would come across that little word, "faith". It occurs no less than 40 times in that book. Faith, faith, faith, faith ... forty times. You would find, to your amazement, perhaps, that it is not found in any other book, of the New Testament, just so often. (Indeed, the nearest approach is the Epistle to the Hebrews in which it occurs 32 times.) We come to the conclusion, therefore, that we could write across the whole Epistle of the Romans one single word - Faith. That is exactly what the book is all about! Was that not the way you started the Christian journey, when you were saved? Is it any wonder God puts it first in your Bible? He expects you to study it first. He expects you to understand it before you go to Ephesians.

So Romans is the book of Faith. That is easy. If you were to come to Thessalonians you would find that the Coming of the Lord is mentioned in chapter 1; the Coming of the Lord is mentioned in chapter 2; the Coming of the Lord is mentioned in chapter 3; then in chapter 4 and also in chapter 5, and you are at the end of I Thessalonians. So you start to read II Thessalonians, and you find that the Coming of the Lord is found in chapter 1, and in chapter 2, and in chapter 3, and you are at the end of II Thessalonians. So the whole of Thessalonians has got to do with His Coming, and there is not a soul who would argue with me on that. I can, therefore, write one word across the whole of Thessalonians - Hope, the Hope of His Coming.

Can you see one word that **must** fit the Ephesians, even if you have never read or studied it, that is, if there is any overall structure in the New Testament books? That one word must fit and will be found in chapter 1, that word which must fit will be found in chapter 2, that word which I must see will be found in chapter 3 and in chapters 4 to 6. Ten times over the verb is used. Ten times over the noun is used. Twenty times altogether the word is used and I am not shocked, when I look at a concordance, to find that there is not another book in the New Testament Scripture which has this word so often. Not one of all Paul's Epistles has this word so often as in the Ephesian Epistle. What could that word be, but Love. It is so plain. I wonder how we have missed it for so long: Faith, Love and Hope. See Figure 1.7.

Rightly Dividing the Word of Truth

It would be an interesting thing, now, to study the last nine books of the New Testament, from the Epistle to the Hebrews

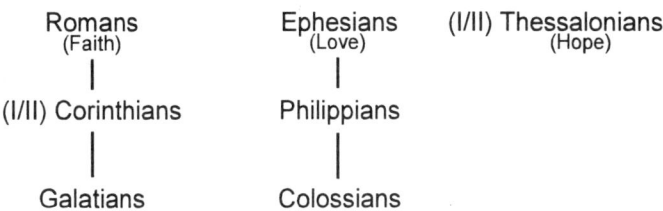

Figure 1.7: **The Balance of Paul's Writings**

to the Book of the Revelation. I am not going to do that, but if I did, I would find, as mentioned above, that the Epistle to the Hebrews is also all about Faith. That is the first book of this group, is it not? The Book of the Revelation, the last book of this group, is all about the Hope of His Coming. In between, you get the little Epistles of John, and they all have got to do with Love. And so the whole pattern repeats itself in this second group of Epistles. See Figure 1.8.

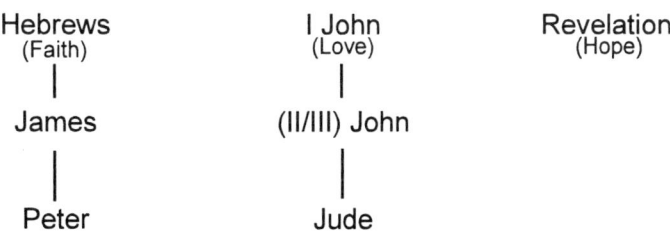

Figure 1.8: **The Balance of Hebrews to Revelation**

Church Principles for Today

If the Book of Romans has got to do with Faith then it would deal with the Cross. Which, of course, it does.

When we turn to this Epistle to the Ephesians, we find that it has got to do with a Mystery. You will find a Mystery in chapter 1, a Mystery in chapter 2, a Mystery in chapter 3, a Mystery in chapter 5 and a Mystery in chapter 6. It has got to do with the Mystery of the Church. Would you notice that the very last verses of the Epistle to the Romans end with a Mystery, which is not explained? The Ephesian Epistle takes that up and expands it. So the Epistle to the Ephesians is the exposition of the Mystery with which the Epistle to the Romans ends and that Mystery has got to do with the Church.

The Book of the Thessalonians has got to do with the future. As we said, the word, "Coming" is mentioned in every chapter and it has got to do with the Lord's Coming for His Church.

So you see there is a broad plan laid out in the order of the books of our New Testament Scriptures (apart from the plan of each individual book, which I will seek to show also in this chapter). So that here we have Faith, Love and Hope; the Cross, the Church, the Coming; Faith that is past, the day I was

Rightly Dividing the Word of Truth

saved; the Church that is present; and Hope that is the future, we are waiting for His Coming.

Further, this Epistle to the Romans has got to do with the individual. It has got to do with you - as if there was not another soul under the canopy of Heaven. Just you. Ephesians is not. Ephesians is the book of the gathering. You will not be surprised to find Thessalonians is the book of the gathering-up, 'caught up to meet Him in the air'. So that one here, and one there, are saved as individuals but one day the Lord will come and take the Church, which is His Body, Home. The order is so plain and so easy to see. See Figure 1.9.

Now, we have learned in life that it is possible for a saint to

Romans - Mystery -	**Ephesians**	**Thessalonians**
- Faith	- Love	- Hope
- Cross	- Church	- Coming
- Past	- Present	- Future
- Individual	- Gathering	- Gathering-up

Figure 1.9: **The Main Themes of Paul's Writings**

make mistakes. He can err. But he can err in one of two different kinds of ways. He can err first of all, if you like, in a moral way. He can steal, that is morally wrong. He can tell lies, that is morally wrong. He can go astray morally. But there is another way in which he can go astray. He can have a misunderstanding of some of the amazing truths of New Testament Scripture and so go astray doctrinally. Which of the two is the more serious? Would you think that the poor person who goes morally astray is in a more serious spiritual state than he who goes astray doctrinally? I want to tell you plainly that of the two, the more serious is doctrinal. It is not very often that the young folk of the Churches are carried away doctrinally. The devil seeks to knock them off morally, but he takes the leaders of the Church, and the teachers of the Local Assembly, and seeks to knock them off doctrinally. Almost all of the gatherings you have ever known, which have suffered in any way, have been divided because of doctrinal error, not moral error. A few, yes, but mostly doctrinal. The history of the Church will show that doctrinal error is very, very serious.

Is there a way that I can doctrinally misunderstand the Epistle to the Romans? Yes! Read Galatians and see that the problem there was that they had misunderstood the Epistle to the

Rightly Dividing the Word of Truth

Romans. If you do not understand the Romans you will fall into the error of Galatia.

The brethren have seen for years that these two books are very similar. They talk about the same thing. For example, when Romans talks about Abraham, it quotes Genesis, chapter 15. When Galatians talks about Abraham, it also quotes Genesis, chapter 15. (When Hebrews talks about Abraham, it quotes Genesis, chapter 22, and, of course, when James talks about Abraham, he quotes Genesis, chapter 22. These two books are also similar.) But there is a difference between Romans and Galatians: Galatia had doctrinal error. You must always watch out for it. If you never want to fall into the doctrinal error of Galatia there is one thing you must do: You must get an understanding of the Epistle to the Romans. It behoves us, therefore, to understand the book that God has put first because, if we do not, there is a possibility that we might fall into the doctrinal error of Galatia.

Then there is that other book, Corinthians. It lies between Romans and Galatians. What is it all about? Moral error! Is it not an interesting thing that in I Corinthians, chapter 5, it says, "a little leaven leaveneth the whole lump"? In Galatians, chapter, 5, it says the very same thing - "a little leaven leaveneth the whole lump". If the doctrinal error of Galatia gets into the Church it will not stop with one person. It will spread to two, and from two to three, and it will not be long until the whole fellowship is affected. That is why there must be Discipline. Is there a particular form of Discipline that deals with this doctrinal error? Yes. (See chapter 7.)

But if it is doctrinal error in Galatians, then what is wrong in Corinthians? Read it. It is not doctrinal now, it is moral error. In I Corinthians, chapter 5, someone is doing something they should not have done but it will not stay confined there. It will not be long till two of the saints are affected, and it will not be long till three are affected, and it will not stop. That is why there must be Discipline. So Discipline brings to rest the doctrinal error of Galatia, and Discipline brings to naught the moral error of Corinth. If I had understood the Roman Epistle, I would never have fallen in Corinth's moral error. Never! That is why I must read, and truly understand, the Epistle to the Romans. Then someone comes along and begins to read Ephesians, but he does not understand it too well. I am not too surprised, as he did not study Romans to begin with! But because he has not understood the truth of Ephesians he falls into

Rightly Dividing the Word of Truth

doctrinal error. Is that corrected anywhere? Yes, in Colossians. The saints, for years, have seen the similarity of Ephesians and Colossians. They are so like one another that one would wonder why, when Ephesians was written, was there any need for Colossians. But the difference is that Ephesians is a pure Church, unadulterated, whereas Colossians has doctrinal error due to the misunderstanding of the Ephesian Epistle.

Is there any cure for that? Yes, Discipline. If Discipline is not exercised it will pass from one believer to two, and from two to three, and from three to four, until it permeates the whole Church. It will not stop until Discipline is introduced.

There is another little letter, Philippians. It comes in between Ephesians and Colossians. What is it all about? Well, the emphasis is not on doctrinal error in chapter 1, nor in chapter 2, nor in chapter 3, nor in chapter 4 and there are only four chapters. There is no Old Testament quotation in chapter 1. There is no Old Testament quotation in chapter 2, nor in chapter 3, nor in chapter 4 and that is it. There is no argument in chapter 1, no arguments in chapter 2, there are none in chapter 3 and there is not one in chapter 4. Then what is this Philippian Epistle all about? What must it be all about? Do I have to tell you? Is it not

Church Principles for Today

plain? Moral error! Two sisters could not agree. (That is only a part of it.) If we were to look at Philippians we would find that Paul is full of joy in chapter 1, he is full of joy in chapter 2, he is full of joy in chapter 3 and he is full of joy in chapter 4. He is joyous in chapter 1, yet he is in jail. He is full of joy in chapter 4, yet he is in need. But at the end of chapter 3, he is weeping. Why? Because he knows that, "a little leaven leaveneth the whole lump". The epistle of joy is turned into an epistle of weeping, because of moral error.

So we see moral error in Corinth, doctrinal error in Galatians, moral error in Philippians and doctrinal error in Colossians: The same order in both groups. See Figure 1.10.

Figure 1.10:   **The Total Balance of Paul's Writings**

Rightly Dividing the Word of Truth

Therefore, it behoves us when we look at all this, that we get a hold of the Epistle to the Romans. We really must. Because the rest of the group traces back to that epistle.

(For a panoramic view of the inter-relationship of all the Books of the Bible, please see Appendix.)

The Epistle to the Romans

What I want to do now is to take this Epistle to the Romans and to structure it for you, so that you can see what way it works and what its thrust is.

We find, firstly, that you can read the whole book, from beginning to end, in 55 minutes. The whole of it. It has 16 chapters, the same as I Corinthians.

You will find that there is a doxology at the end of chapter 8, then there is another doxology at the end of chapter 11 and there is a third doxology at the end of the book. The Holy Spirit of God has kindly divided the book into three parts: Chapters 1 to 8 form the first part; chapters 9, 10 and 11 form the second part and chapters 12 through to 16 form the third part. It is divinely divided.

If I could understand chapters 1 to 8, do you know what I would say? I would say, "Who shall lay any thing to the charge of God's elect? It is God that justifieth." (Romans chapter, 8:33-39) Then, if I understood chapters 1 to 8, I would say, "Who is he that condemneth? It is Christ that died." Then I would say, "Who shall separate us from the love of Christ?" Then I would say, 'No one in Heaven, or Earth, or Hell.' Why? Because of the doctrine of chapters 1, 2, 3, 4, 5, 6, 7 and 8. Would you like to understand these chapters? Would you like, at the end of those eight chapters, to be able to say, with a true heart, "Who shall lay any thing to the charge of God's elect? ... Who is he that condemneth? ... Who shall separate us from the love of Christ?" Do you know that there is not one word from Heaven, and not one from Earth and none from 'the Deep' to answer the question? Why? Chapters 1 to 8 tells you the whole story. Can you see why you must understand them? There is no use in reading that doxology until you see why it is there and what it means, and you cannot do that unless you understand those chapters.

Chapter 9 opens a new sort of arrangement and so we come

Rightly Dividing the Word of Truth

to the next doxology at the end of chapter 11. If I were to understand chapters 9, 10 and 11, do you know what I would do? I would proclaim this doxology but, mark you, the doxology at the end of chapter 8 would not suit here, because there is a different thing being taught. What I would have to do when I came to the end of chapter 11, would be to say, "Oh, the depth of the riches both of the wisdom and knowledge of God! How unsearchable are his judgments, and his ways past finding out!" (Romans chapter, 11:33-36). But you will never be able to say that truthfully, in your heart, unless you have understood chapters 9, 10 and 11.

If I understand the next five chapters, I will be able to shout the doxology at the end of the book. Then I will never fall into Corinth's moral error, nor will I fall into Galatia's doctrinal error.

(So, after having studied, and understood, the Romans, I can, perhaps, bypass those Epistles of Corinthians and Galatians and start to study the Epistle to the Ephesians and seek to understand what it is all about!

There you would find that chapters 1, 2 and 3 are doctrinal.

Church Principles for Today

That is where the Colossians went astray. You would find that chapters 4, 5 and 6 are practical, or moral, if you like, and that is where the Philippians went astray.

Then, after I have understood Ephesians it is then time to go to the Book of Thessalonians.

I have got to understand these books in their order, that is why God has put them that way.)

We have found that the first eight chapters of the Epistle to the Romans form a section. Further study shows that at the very beginning of this section, God shows us that we have a spiritual problem. God tells us exactly what that spiritual problem is. He goes into it in detail, in chapter 1, and explains it. But you cannot solve it. Indeed, all the brethren put together could not solve it. Not even the angels in Heaven, nor even the seraphim, with all their intelligence, could solve this problem. The devil could not solve it, he would not want to. All the intelligentsia and the powers in high places together could not solve it. It is a problem that is beyond solution. It just cannot be solved. Then God comes in, in chapter 3, and solves it. Is that not wonderful? Would you like to know how He solves it? Would you love to know what the problem is? Then, read chapters 1 to 5.

Rightly Dividing the Word of Truth

I am beginning to see already the reason for that doxology at the end of chapter 8: "Who shall lay any thing to the charge of God's elect?" God has solved the problem. "Who can separate us from the love of Christ?" God has solved the problem. "Who can condemn us now?" There is no answer. Do you know why? Because God solved my spiritual problem.

It would be a good thing, therefore, to study the Epistle to the Romans, chapters 1, 2, 3, 4, 5, right up to verse 11, and understand, not only, my first and most fundamental spiritual problem, but why God puts it first.

But God has another spiritual problem which He wants to tell me about. After He solves this first spiritual problem, I find that I have a second one! I always thought there was only one, but when I read the Epistle to the Romans I find I have two. A problem which I cannot solve. A problem that all the angels in Heaven could not solve. All the Christians on Earth could not solve it either. It is an insoluble problem. Then God comes down. Do you know what He does? He solves it! Would you like to know how He solves it? The end of chapter 5 explains what the problem is, in detail, and if I go right through to chapter 7, verse 6, I will find how God solves it.

Church Principles for Today

Then I find I have yet another spiritual problem! I thought I had only one. Now, I have three! What is it now? I want to tell you something, and I wish the dear saints would understand it. Of course, I would long for all the saints to understand how God solved that first spiritual problem; indeed, I would long for all the saints to understand how He solved the second spiritual problem as well; but, I long with all my heart for the saints to understand how He solved this third spiritual problem, because it is worse than the second, and it, in turn, is worse than the first. Do you know, there is no power in Heaven, Earth or Hell that could solve that third spiritual problem? So what happens? God comes down and solves it!

Can you see what is happening in the Epistle to the Romans? Problem number 1 cannot be solved. God solves it. Problem number 2 cannot be solved. God solves it. Problem number 3 cannot be solved. God solves it. There are no problems left, because God has solved them all. Therefore, we shout with joy, "Who shall separate us from the love of Christ?" Who shall condemn us? Who can? No one! God has solved all our problems.

Then, all problems are over, are they not? Not yet. There is another one, and chapter 9 starts off with this fourth spiritual problem and if it is not solved, then the consequences are very, very serious. I find that the solutions to my first, three spiritual problems are null and void if God cannot answer, or solve, this fourth spiritual problem. You could not do it. The angels in Heaven could not do it, so God comes down and He solves it. And by the time you come to the end of that section, and see God's solution to that problem, I declare that you will, with the apostle, break out and cry, 'O, how Thy ways are beyond finding out,' for you will be amazed at what God has done.

Can you see the order, the structure, the thrust, of the book? See Table 1.3.

Doctrinal	- chapters 1-5:11	My first spiritual problem solved by God.
	- chapters 5:12-7:6	My second spiritual problem solved by God.
	- chapters 7:7-8:30	My third spiritual problem solved by God.
	- chapters 8:31-39	Doxology
	- chapters 9:1-11:32	A fourth spiritual problem solved by God.
	- chapters 11:33-36	Doxology

Table 1.3: The first half of the Epistle to the Romans

Church Principles for Today

Finally, you come then to what is called the practical, or moral, part of the book. It starts at chapter 12, with the words, 'Therefore, I beseech you'. Why does he say, "therefore"? Well, would you look at what God did for you in your first spiritual problem? Would you look at what God did for you in your second spiritual problem? You could do nothing about it. He did everything. Do you not see what He did for you in your third spiritual problem? Do you see what He did in the fourth spiritual problem? He did all that for you. Would you like to do something for Him? 'Therefore - present yourselves to Him wholly!'

One word could be written right across chapter 12 - dedication, or consecration, if you like. One word could be written over chapter 13 - subordination, to the laws of the land. Over chapter 14 could be written one word - toleration. I wish we knew something about that in our Churches! Over the fifteenth chapter could be written one word - evangelisation. Over the sixteenth chapter could be written - accommodation. See Table 1.4.

Chapter 12. Dedication	- my heart is right.
Chapter 13. Subordination -	- no one, out there, can lay any charge against my testimony
Chapter 14. Toleration -	- everyone in the assembly has the best to say about me, whatever they may think.
Chapter 15. Evangelisation	- Do you not think I should go out and evangelise?
Chapter 16. Accommodation -	the day will come whenever I receive that "Well done, thou good and faithful servant ... enter thou into the joy of thy Lord." (Matthew chapter, 25:21).

Table 1.4: The second half of the Epistle to the Romans

Then, at the close of this final section, it is no wonder that in chapter 16, verses 25 - 27, we have that third doxology:

"Now to him that is of power to stablish you according to my gospel, and the preaching of Jesus Christ, according to the revelation of the mystery, which was kept secret since the world began, But now is made manifest, and by the scriptures of the prophets, according to the commandment of the everlasting God, made known to all nations for the obedience of faith: To God only wise, be glory through Jesus Christ for ever. Amen."

Church Principles for Today

So we have come to the end of the basic structure of the epistles of Paul and, in particular, the thrust of the Epistle to the Romans, as examples of elementary Bible study. Now, it is up to the reader to look for the above spiritual problems and to see just what they were and how the Lord has solved them.

Chapter 2

The Church and the Churches

In these chapters, we are discussing very interesting although, at times, difficult subjects. I am not seeking to exhort, that is not what I set out to do, but rather to explain the fundamentals of Church gatherings, as laid out in Scripture.

My desire is that, as a result of this exercise, we will all be able to understand God's will, for our coming together, more fully.

Church Principles for Today

Therefore, for the subject of, 'The Church and the Churches' our reading is:

The Epistle to the Ephesians, chapter 5, verses 25 - 33.

"Husbands, love your wives, even as Christ also loved the church, and gave himself for it; That he might sanctify and cleanse it with the washing of water by the word, That he might present it to himself a glorious church, not having spot, or wrinkle, or any such thing; but that it should be holy and without blemish. So ought men to love their wives as their own bodies. He that loveth his wife loveth himself. For no man ever yet hated his own flesh; but nourisheth and cherisheth it, even as the Lord the church: For we are members of his body, of his flesh, and of his bones. For this cause shall a man leave his father and mother, and shall be joined unto his wife, and they two shall be one flesh. This is a great mystery: but I speak concerning Christ and the church. Nevertheless let everyone of you in particular so love his wife even as himself; and the wife see that she reverence her husband."

Then, in the Book of the Revelation, chapter 1, verses 19 and 20:

The Church and the Churches

"Write the things which thou has seen, and the things which are, and the things which shall be hereafter; The mystery of the seven stars which thou sawest in my right hand, and the seven golden candlesticks. The seven stars are the angels of the seven churches: and the seven candlesticks which thou sawest are the seven churches."

Then in Joshua, chapter 20, verses 1 - 9:

"The Lord also spake unto Joshua, saying, Speak to the children of Israel, saying, Appoint out for you cities of refuge, whereof I spake unto you by the hand of Moses: That the slayer that killeth any person unawares and unwittingly may flee thither: and they shall be your refuge from the avenger of blood. And when he that doth flee unto one of those cities shall stand at the entering of the gate of the city, and shall declare his cause in the ears of the elders of that city, they shall take him into the city unto them, and give him a place, that he may dwell among them. And if the avenger of blood pursue after him, then they shall not deliver the slayer up into his hand; because he smote his neighbour unwittingly, and hated him not beforetime. And he shall dwell in that city, until he stand before the congregation for judgment, and until the death of the high priest that shall be in those days: then shall the slayer return, and come unto his own city, and unto his own house, unto the city from whence he fled. And they appointed Kedesh in Galilee in mount Naphtali, and Shechem in mount Ephraim, and Kirjath-arba, which is Hebron, in the mountain of Judah. And on the other side Jordan by Jericho eastward, they assigned Bezer in the wilderness upon the plain out of the tribe of Reuben, and Ramoth in Gilead out of the tribe of Gad, and Golan in Bashan out of the tribe of Manasseh. These were the cities appointed for all the children of Israel, and for the stranger that sojourneth among them, that whosoever killeth any person at unawares might flee thither, and not die by the hand of the avenger of blood, until he stood before the congregation."

The Introduction

In the last chapter we took a little look at the Epistles of the New Testament and we saw that they were certainly not placed in any haphazard order. While we took a brief look at the chronological order of the writings, we found that the actual order of the books, in the New Testament, was altogether different. We saw that although the Epistle to the Romans was written after the Epistles to the Thessalonians, yet in our Bible it comes before them. We saw, in our simple studies, that one of the reasons for this, is that God intended that we should understand the Epistle to the Romans first. Romans is altogether and absolutely fundamental to our knowledge of all other books and every one of us, and Gospel preachers in particular, should have a sound working knowledge of its teachings.

The Church and the Churches

We saw that the first part of that beautiful book has got to do with spiritual problems, which we all have had. Spiritual problems which cannot be solved by man. Spiritual problems which are so complex that all the saints together could not solve them. Spiritual problems which are so complex that all the angels in Heaven could not solve them. They were left altogether and absolutely for God to solve. So having come to the conclusion that as it was God who had dealt with our spiritual problems, then we could rest assured that He had done it properly.

We are told, 'It is not by any works of righteousness which we have done but according to His grace and mercy that He saved us.' Therefore, we were able to say in Romans, chapter 8, "Who shall separate us from the love of Christ?" We were able to cry out with joy, 'Who shall condemn us now?' We are able to cry with joy, 'Who is he that can lay anything to the charge of God's elect?' The answer to all three questions is that nothing, and no one, can touch us – for God has solved all our spiritual problems.

Now that we are saved, we look at the next major book that comes along and it is the Epistle to the Ephesians. We saw, in our simple remarks, that it has got to do with something which was called, 'The Church'.

Now, in this chapter, I want to deal with this subject of the Universal Church, and compare it to the Churches - those local gatherings of Christian men and women. Our subject, therefore, is extensive and it would take a whole book, I suppose, to go over all the things which are so surely believed amongst us. Yet, in a sense, the title of our subject has narrowed the field because the question is asked almost in the title, What does our gathering together mean? What I want to do, therefore, is to study why we are to gather together.

The Godhead

In the study of what we call the God-head, we would find from the Scriptures, that there are three Persons. Each of these three Persons is as distinct as any three individual people. It is not an amalgamation of three entities in one Person. The Godhead consists of three Persons, each utterly and absolutely distinct. Now, I did not say that there are three Gods. That would be a denial of the whole of Scripture. There is only one God, but God consists of three Persons.

The Church and the Churches

In Genesis, God said, 'Let Us ... let Us make man in Our own image'. So away back in the very opening chapters of our Bible, almost in the very opening verses, there is a hint at the fact that while there is one God, in the God-head, there are distinct Persons.

We have come to call each of these three Persons by different names. We refer to God, the Father; we refer to God, the Son; and we refer to God, the Holy Spirit.

If we were being academic, I think we could show that this is not the right way to say it, because it gives a wrong implication. Far, far better, if I was to say that the Father is God: That is true; the Son is God, the same God: That is true; the Spirit is God, the same God: That is true. So while there are three Persons, there is only one God.

That is, perhaps, beyond our understanding. What mind could comprehend the God-head, anyway? We are told, are we not, that eternity itself will never be able to exhaust the Person of Christ, never mind, the God-head?

I remember when I was a little child, in the faith, my beloved brethren taught me not to divide the deity and not to try to divide the God-head. Oh, I know what they were referring to, all right. I can see their care. But we must go back to the Scriptures and see that they make a clear distinction between the Father, and the Son, and the Spirit of God.

Who was it that kneeled in the Garden of Gethsemane? Was it the Spirit of God? Now, you know it was not. It was the Son. Who was it that was nailed to the cross, at Calvary? Was it the Father? No, it was the Son. Who was it that laid upon Christ the iniquity of us all? Was it the Spirit? Was it not the Father? Was it not God? Consequently we must see a clear distinction between the three Persons of the God-head and ever remember that while three, only one God.

If we could use the Scripture perhaps slightly out of context, there was a cry that went throughout Heaven, in eternity past (if I may call it that). The cry was, 'Who will go, who will go for Us?' Us? Yes, the God-head. Go where? What for? So that God could fill Heaven with people like His Son!

I remember years ago, when we had the three children still at home. We had our first-born, a boy; the second-born, a little

The Church and the Churches

girl; the third-born, a little boy. We could not say we loved the girl more than the boys, nor any one of the boys more than the girl. We loved them all exactly the same. But the youngest of them did gave us extreme delight, especially his Mummy. One day, she took him, and hugged him, and squeezing him, said out of the pure joy in her soul, "I wish the house was filled with sons just like you". I could see what she meant. The child gave her such delight that she wanted the house to be filled with sons like him.

It is clear that sometime, somewhere, God viewed His Son, the Lord Jesus, and in His sovereign councils, which defy our understanding, He purposed that, one day, heaven would be peopled with sons, just like His own. So, God sat down to do a little bit of planning, and the Lord Jesus sat down with Him, and the Spirit sat down as well. This was before there was an Earth; before there was a Heaven; before there was an angel; before there was a seraph; before there was a cherub; before there was a devil; before there was anything at all. In the council chambers of 'Somewhere', the God-head sat down to plan.

Do not say that, that 'Somewhere' was Heaven, for that is not so. Heaven is not eternal. God made Heaven and before

Church Principles for Today

Heaven was, He was, and there was nothing else with Him. God, alone, was at the beginning.

How is our God then going to fill Heaven with sons like His own? Who could have planned it but God? It meant the creation of this great universe as we know it. It meant the creation of a man. It meant the creation of a woman. It meant, in the permissive will of God, a fall. It meant all these things.

By and by, in answer to God's question, the Person of God's Son said, 'Here am I. I will go to Earth, according to God's plan'. In the Epistle to the Colossians we read these words, 'And it pleased Him, that in Him should all fullness dwell'. Pleased who? It pleased the deity. It pleased the God-head. It pleased the Father. It pleased the Spirit. It pleased the Son. It pleased God, that in the Person of the Lord Jesus Christ, all fullness should dwell. And He came to Earth.

It meant His living. It meant His dying. Then, one day, the Lord Jesus Christ went up, and up, right into Heaven, from whence He came, and after He went up, the Spirit of God came right down to Earth.

The Church and the Churches

The Lord Jesus Christ went up, in Acts, chapter 1, and He has been there ever since, and He will not come back again until I Thessalonians, chapter 4. The Spirit of God came down, in Acts, chapter 2, and His headquarters has been on Earth, this last 2,000 years.

The Church

What happened when the Spirit of God came down? Oh, He came down to do a number of wonderful things. One of those is that He came from Heaven, to give us our New Testament Scripture. That could be proved. There are many other reasons, but the one that interests me is this: He came down that He might form what is known, in the New Testament, as the Church, which is His Body.

The Gospel of the Lord Jesus Christ is going out to the whole wide world today, and from the millions of people on Earth, God is calling one here and one there, by His grace. Men and women are hearing the Gospel message and responding, and their spiritual problems are being taken away by God and they are being saved. They have been getting saved since the Acts of the Apostles, chapter 2, right through those Dark Ages, right up until now, and will continue to do so, until the moment that the Lord comes, in I Thessalonians, chapter 4. God has been calling out of the nations a people for His name and He is going to make them all sons.

Not so very long ago, my wife and I were talking about these things and I said, "How gracious God has been to us". I can go back to my school days and think of all the pupils that sat beside me and as far as I know only one, other than myself, is saved. How gracious God was to us!

I can remember so well, when I was a little child, of eight years old, I fell in school and cut my knee and I was left with a scar, the thickness and length of your finger. In some conference meetings in Belfast, a year or so ago, a brother came over to me and said, "Brother Jennings, don't you know me?" I replied that I did not. He said, "You and I went to school together. I remember the day you fell and cut your knee".

And I thought that nobody had been saved, but me. God, in His grace, had saved another in the class and, perhaps, when I get Home I will find that He has called out from my class, not only that brother and me, but maybe them all. God has called

The Church and the Churches

one here and one there. What for? To fill Heaven with sons like His own.

As you look now, people might never realise that you are a son of God, but just wait until God has finished with you and then take a look. When He has finished with all of us, and gets us Home, I want to tell you, we will look like a son of God then.

So, God is calling out of these nations a great company for His name, which is the Body of Christ, namely, the Church: Made up of every soul who is saved, wherever they may go on Sunday, whatever their colour, whatever their class, whatever their creed.

How many millions will be in it? I do not know. However, in order for God to help us understand this great concept, He calls that company of people by a number of different names. I want to look at those names and try to teach something of the very nature of this Church, which is His Body.

For the sake of clarity I am going to draw a table and refer to this Universal Church simply as, 'The Church'. Everything un-

Church Principles for Today

derneath this heading, has got to do with that great company of people, of whom we have been referring. Next to this heading we will put another, namely, 'The Churches'. We are going to see the similarities and differences between these. See Table 2.1.

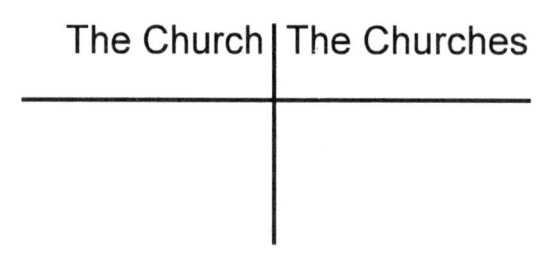

The Church	The Churches

Table 2.1:   **The Church and the Churches**

The very first thing I want to clarify, therefore, is that the Church is not a building. It is not something built of bricks and mortar. In fact, this is that Church of which the Lord Jesus Himself said in Matthew, chapter 16, "I will build my church". We want to learn something about that Church and the first thing is that it is not a place where people come together to worship. We may call that building a Church, but God does not. When God speaks of, 'The Church', He is thinking rather of a vast, vast group of people. A people which is, for you and me, altogether without number.

The Church and the Churches

When we think of this vast company of people, we might wonder why God ever formed it. Why did He ever plan that there should be this thing called, 'The Church'? Why should He call people from every nation, kindred, tongue and tribe by His grace? That is the whole story of the Ephesian Epistle. If we would take up that beautiful book we would begin to find out just why God ever designed this Church, which is His Body.

The very first reason, and to me the most beautiful, is what we find, in Ephesians, chapter 1. There is coming a day when the Lord Jesus Christ is going to rule in Millennial Glory. Then, away beyond that there will be the new Earth, and a new Heaven with all its constellations, whatever they may be called, and Christ shall rule supreme, as the Head over all things.

Tell me, who is He going to use to do the ruling? He is going to rule it through the instrumentality of His Church: 'For the world to come,' says Hebrews, chapter 2, 'is not given unto angels to rule, but unto men.' 'The day is coming,' says the Apostle Paul, in I Corinthians, chapter 6, 'when we shall judge the world.' 'The day is coming,' says I Corinthians, chapter 6, 'when we shall judge angels.' There is going to be a delegation of authority.

Today, the Lord Jesus is calling out of the nations of Earth a people for His name, that through the Church He will rule the universe that is still to come, as well as in Millennial Glory. What a wonderful thing!

Mind you, if you study the Judgment Seat of Christ you will begin to understand, that we cannot all have the same place in Millennial Glory, can we? We cannot all be Prime Ministers, can we? There must be that descending order of delegation of authority. At the Judgment Seat of Christ, the Lord is going to delegate His authority to every member of the Church, in direct proportion to how we behaved ourselves in our life, down here. So God is training us, all of us. He is training us for the authority He is going to give us in that coming great day. We find that in Ephesians, chapter 1.

We find also in the Epistle to the Ephesians, chapter 1, at the close of the chapter, that although the Lord Jesus Christ fills all things, yet there is a void. That is impossible for us to understand but, 'He that filleth all things, the Person of the Lord Je-

The Church and the Churches

sus Christ, Himself must be filled'. The Lord Jesus is going to be made complete by the Church!

We can understand that more clearly, perhaps, if we go to Adam and Eve in the Garden of Eden. Adam was the head at the beginning; he was monarch of all he surveyed, but he was alone. Then, one day, God took him and gave him a wife. A helpmete for him, that she might be with him in his domain. Would you like to understand Ephesians, chapter 1, verse 22, where it says, "And hath put all things under his feet, and gave him to be the head over all things to the Church, Which is his body, the fullness of him that filleth all in all"? This Body, being His fullness in a coming day, when in that great, vast domain, God is going to use it to help Him in its administration. That is Heaven.

Some may say, 'I thought Heaven was a city with golden streets, where we would sit on golden thrones, before a golden mantelpiece, playing a golden harp. It is no such thing!

The eternal Heaven is going to be a place of immense activity, where Christ is the Head of all administration. It is a place which He is going to administer through this company of believers that are baptized in the Holy Spirit. That is why He is calling out a nation of people for His Name. That is why He went to such trouble. Some of us will be the Prime Minister, if you wish. Some of us will be the Ministers of State. But, whether we be high up or low down, everyone will have his, or her, part therein. That is why God made this pattern.

Then, in chapter 5, of this Ephesian Epistle, we find that a man was altogether complete of himself and yet in a sense he was not. He needed his wife. So with the Lord Jesus Christ, He that filleth all things, will need the Church, in that day which is still to come.

Then, we would find a most amazing thing, in chapter 2, of the Epistle to the Ephesians: Throughout the ages of eternity God is going to display the very riches of His grace. How? Through the Church. Sometimes I am amazed at that. When the angels of Heaven, and the cherubim, and the seraphim, and all the other families of Heaven see, in Heaven, human beings, all brought there through no works of their own, but by grace, and see Heaven filled with sons of God, like unto His own Son, they will begin to see clearly, for the first time, the riches of the grace of Almighty God. Angels have been with God a long,

The Church and the Churches

long time. They have not learned all there is to know, yet. There are some things which the angels have never yet been able to understand. They have never been able to understand, even yet, the riches of His grace. But as the ages roll their course, and we go beyond the Veil and into that Eternal State, God is going to display, He is going to show, to all those families in Heaven, the depths and wonders of His grace through the object lesson of, 'The Church'.

That is why it says in Ephesians, chapter 2, 'Not of works, lest any man should boast. It is by grace are you saved'. That is not a Gospel story. If we keep to the context, the reason why that Scripture is there, is so that on that great day, God might show the wonders of His grace. An ever unfolding wonder of His grace through the Church. Why has God called these people? Why has He called me? Why has He called us? Because He wants me to be an object lesson to all the powers of Heaven.

Then, also in Ephesians, chapter 3, it says, "... now unto the principalities and powers in heavenly places might be known by the church (the Body) the manifold wisdom of God." What does this mean? In the very day in which we live, the angels above are looking down with mystic wonder upon this Church.

Church Principles for Today

So often we hear people saying that this is the age when nothing big is being done. We think of our little circumspect meeting and of how little we have done and are doing now. But wait! Take your eye off your Local Church and get your eyes on the world globe and then ask yourself what God is doing. He is working in Russia in a way you know nothing about. He is working in Palestine in a way you know nothing about. There never was a day when the Gospel of Christ was more proclaimed than today. And the angels of God are looking down in absolute wonder at the wisdom of God. Then we have the audacity to say that this is the age of small things, and that God is not revealing Himself, as in past days!

Therefore, we should be very careful of the way we behave ourselves. Those angels which have been with Him for thousands of years. You would have thought they would have known everything of God that had to be known. That is not so! Day-by-day the angels are learning the very wisdom of God. How? Through His Church. The Church is, even today, an object lesson for them. That is why, I repeat, we ought to behave ourselves exceedingly carefully.

Then, you will find in Ephesians, chapter 4, that God wants

The Church and the Churches

this Body to grow, just as little children grow. When the little children are born their heads are very big! I think you know that. There is a physical reason for that, but God uses that as a wonderful example. You see, there is nothing wrong with the head of the baby, it is the body that is the problem. The body is small. A physical reason? Yes! But by-and-by the body begins to fill out, until finally the body is in proportion to the head. What you could say is, 'The body has grown to suit the size of the head'. This is exactly what God longs for this Body, which is the Church: That we might grow up into Him, in order that we might be able to fit the task that lies before us, more perfectly.

Imagine, these days in which we live, are days of discipline and schooling, looking forward to a great universe, to an Age which is to come, in which God is going to use you and use me. He is claiming us and He wants us to grow that we might be more perfectly fitted, I repeat, to do our job in that great Age.

It is not my intention to go into the whole Ephesian Epistle, and give an exposition of all the reasons why the Church has ever been called out by God. But there is one more I would like to mention.

Church Principles for Today

When we come to Ephesians, chapter 5, what had the Lord in mind when He talked about husbands and wives? He was thinking of that day when He would join Himself to that vast company of people by an indissoluble bond. A bond so exceedingly wonderful that He refers to it in similar terms as a marriage tie. That group of persons with whom He is going to associate Himself, forever, is the Church. Some day, one day, He is going to take us all and present us to Himself as, 'a Bride', without blemish, or without spot, or without any such thing.

We see, therefore, from each of those five chapters, of Ephesians, some concept of this Body of believers. This is represented in Figure 2.1.

        Chapter 1 - Administration

        Chapter 2 - Displaying God's grace

        Chapter 3 - Displaying God's wisdom

        Chapter 4 - Fitting for future/eternal rule

        Chapter 5 - The Bride of Christ

Figure 2.1:   **Reasons for the Body of Christ, in Ephesians**

These, however, are only a few of the reasons why God ever

The Church and the Churches

thought of saving people from every kindred, tongue, nation and tribe.

The Church - Its names

To help us to understand what this great company of people means to God, He uses certain similes, while at other times He uses metaphors. Sometimes He calls this great, vast company of people as we have seen, 'a Body'. He does that in Ephesians, chapters 1 and 2.

Why? What could He be thinking of? Well, if I consider my body, I think I can understand it all. To illustrate this to some beloved saints, I once mentioned that if someone came into my garage, one day, and saw me working at the vice with one foot in the air, they would ask,

"Mr. Jennings, what is wrong with your leg? Is it sore?"

"No, no, it is not sore."

"Have you not got a sore knee?"

"No, no, I have not a sore knee, at all."

"What is wrong with your leg then?"

"Nothing, it has just fallen out with the rest of the body."

"Well", you would say, "That is preposterous."

Church Principles for Today

You would never dream of your leg falling out with the other leg. My whole body works together as one. Is that not what God wants of all His saints? Oh, how He longs for it! He wants us all to work together like a body: No schisms, no divisions.

What sort of a silly man would you think me to be, if you came into the garage and I had my thumb in the vice and I had the hack-saw in my hand?

"What are you doing Mr. Jennings?"

"I am cutting off this member. I do not agree with that thumb anymore. The sooner I get rid of that thumb, the better."

"Cut off your thumb?! But, that is a member of your body."

God does not want members cut off, does He? But I tell you, we do it! We are the best of surgeons, at times. We cut off members of the Body, right, left and centre. Oh, how dare we!

Further, sometimes we hear that a member, or a group, has cut itself off! But that is equally preposterous. How could my thumb cut itself off from my hand. It is impossible. God intended that there should be no schism in the great Body. He wants us all to work together.

The Church and the Churches

Why did God do all this? What is His purpose? What did He have in mind? We will see, in chapter 3, that He took great care to show the Jews that the Samaritans, the Gentiles and the disciples of John are all going to be in this Body. Why? Well, we have noticed that one of the reasons God calls it a Body is because there are going to be no divisions. None at all. We might squabble in the Local Church, and one Assembly might be upset with the Church up the street, but I want to tell you straight, that in God's estimation there are no divisions. It does not matter where I go, or where I hang my hat! God sees every one of us in exactly the same light: The Spirit is in us and we are in the Spirit! God has done all He can (I am speaking carefully and reverently), to show us that there should be no schism. That is why He calls it a Body. Reason number one: No schisms.

Every member in a body should work in perfect harmony with the others. This is what God is seeking to teach: All these persons, who are so different to one another before salvation, are now made one, by the coming of the Spirit.

If I were to look at this body of mine for a moment or two, I would ask, from where does the control come? It comes from my head! Who directs my hand to do this, or that, or directs my foot to do this or that? Where do all the directions come from? The head!

Who is the Head of this Church, which is His Body? The oversight? Tut, tut! The Head of that Body, is Christ. He is the controlling factor and there is not a soul on the face of this Earth should dare ever give messages to the Body of Christ. He is the Head and through the joints and marrows He sends nourishment to every single member of His Body.

Another one of the reasons why God calls it a Body is because it is through a body that a man expresses himself. If I did not have my hands how could I express myself, how could I write? If I had no tongue I would not be much good at teaching. So by my body I express myself and so also does God express Himself – through His Body – which is the Church.

Not only that, but we know that a body grows - then so also does the Church. Not growing in a sense of adding members to it but, if we were to read the Ephesian Epistle, chapter 3, what God is looking for is a development of the members of His Body. He wants us to grow from little children, from toddlers and babes, through young manhood, into fathers.

The Church and the Churches

The reason for this is because one day long, long ago God made a beautiful Earth. After that, He put it into the hands of a man who introduced sin to it. God is not going to do that again. He is going to make the man first, before He makes a new Earth. When He has called out from the nations of this Earth a people that He calls His Church, and has trained them, and disciplined them, and watched them grow as a body would grow, then when He has prepared the men, He will then give to them the new Earth.

So God sometimes refers to this great Church, as a Body.

There is too much in that to deal with in two or three paragraphs, however, it is considered in greater detail, in chapter 3.

Then, in John, chapter 10, He calls it, 'A Flock'. The Lord Jesus speaks there of the Nation of Israel and He says, 'There are other sheep which are not of the Jewish fold, those I must bring that there may be one great Flock'. That Flock is the Church. He calls it a Body, at times, because it grows. He calls it a Body, at times, because it has members working harmoniously together. He calls it a Body, at times, because the Spirit of God dwells in it. He calls it a Body, at times, because it is the way God expresses Himself. But sometimes He calls it a Flock.

Church Principles for Today

Why? Because it needs guidance and tending. Is that not a beautiful thing?

I remember one of the brethren, a long time ago, saying,' Abel was a shepherd and the lamb died for its shepherd. But the Person of the Lord Jesus with regards to His Flock is altogether different, for it was there that the Shepherd died for the Flock'. So sometimes God calls the Church, a Flock.

Tell me, who is the Shepherd? Oh, that is the group of men who govern the meeting. Tut, tut! The Head of the Body, is Christ and the Shepherd of this Flock, is Christ.

We also read, in Ephesians, chapter 2, that He calls it, 'A Temple'. Now the idea there is altogether different to that of the Body, or the Flock. He called it a Body because through it He could express Himself. He called it a Flock, because He died for it and He wants to care and tend for it. But He calls it a Temple because to Him it is altogether holy and He wants to inhabit it.

The Spirit of God dwells in this beautiful Temple. In a world

The Church and the Churches

of sin, and shame, it is 'the place' where there is holiness, it is 'the place' where men worship God, where they draw near to Him. When God thinks of this great company of people which He has gathered out, He says, 'Now there is a place in which I can dwell, and where I can dwell in peace'. Where? In the Church. Why? Because it is a Temple – a place of holiness.

God is determined that everyone in this Temple will, one day, be holy, but He also wants us to be holy while upon this Earth. Indeed, He will do everything in His power to make us holy. Indeed, we would find, if we read the Epistle to the Romans, that God has already done everything that is required to make every single individual of this Universal Church holy, and the reason is because He wants to dwell amongst us. In fact, there is a day coming, according to the Book of the Revelation, chapter 21, when the Seer looks up to Heaven and sees a Tabernacle of God coming down. What is this Tabernacle? It is the Temple.

Then sometimes He calls it, 'A House'. Now that is serious, but He does. In the Epistle to the Hebrews, chapter 3, God calls it, 'a House'. Mind you, a house in Holy Scripture has always got to do with God's governmental dealings with people. Do not think that you can be saved by sovereign grace and be looked upon as the Body of Christ, as the Flock, as the Temple, without also being looked upon as the House!

Therefore, we are not surprised, when we go to the Epistle to the Hebrews, chapter 12, that as little children, in the home, we sometimes have to bear the rod! We will see more of that when we look at the Lord's Supper, in chapter 6, and Assembly Discipline in chapter 7. The House is where God rules supreme.

It is called,' A Mystery', in Ephesians, chapter 5. Why? Because the like of it was never known before.

Does that not give you a fundamental reason for saying that the Church had its inception in the Acts of the Apostles, chapter 2? It could never have been called, a 'Mystery', otherwise!

The like of this was never known, in Old Testament times. It was altogether something that was bound up in the very heart and mind of God and, consequently, God calls it, 'a Mystery'. A Mystery, in the New Testament, is something which was once hidden but is now revealed.

The Church and the Churches

Then, just one more name to complete our study of this Universal Church. In Ephesians, chapter 5, He calls it, 'My Bride'. That we have briefly discussed earlier in the chapter. But why should He call it, a Bride? Because He wants to control it? I should think not. He calls it His Bride because He loves it. The day is coming when He wants to be joined indissolubly to the Bride. The Person of the Lord Jesus Christ died for His Bride and one day He is going to be joined to her, at that great Marriage Supper of the Lamb, at that great Marriage Feast, up above. Black people and yellow, red people and white, everyone of them saved by grace and He says, 'Look at them all, they are My Bride'.

Why does He call the Church by so many names? Is it not all the same thing? Yes , but He is looking at it in different ways. When He says, 'My Body', He means no schisms, all united; 'My Flock', He cares and defends them; 'My Temple', holiness is in His mind; 'My House', discipline is in His mind; 'A Mystery', something hidden in His heart; 'My Bride', He loves her.

As far as the Church is concerned then, we see that God sometimes helps us to understand what it means to Him; helps us to appreciate in our hearts what He wants to see in it when

He calls it by these beautiful names. If I were to describe all the things that God calls it, I would need a diagram going the whole way down the page, but I have chosen those six for a specific purpose, which you will see before long.

Table 2.2 shows, therefore, some of the many names attributed to that vast company of redeemed people, from the Day of Pentecost, in the Acts of the Apostles, chapter 2, until the day the Lord Jesus comes to take us Home, to be with Himself, in I Thessalonians, chapter 4.

This Church, has never been seen by anyone in its entirety. No one has ever seen the whole Body. No one has ever seen the whole Flock. No one has ever seen the whole Temple. But there is a day coming when we will be able to see it all and that will be when the Lord Jesus comes for His people. When He takes this Flock, this Temple, this House, this Church, when He takes it all up, to be with Himself.

I am going to be there because I am a member of the Body; I am in the Church. Sometimes I have thought, however, if I

The Church and the Churches

	The Church (Matt. 16)	The Churches (Matt. 18)
Body	(Eph., 1,2)	
Flock	(Jhn., 10)	
Temple	(Eph., 2)	
House	(Heb., 3)	
Mystery	(Eph., 5)	
Bride	(Eph., 5)	

Table 2.2:   **Various Names for the Universal Church**

could only stand aside on that great day (I will, of course, not be able to), just for a moment or two, and watch the graves be opened; watch the bodies of all those that are lying therein being raised with that new body, like unto the Body of His Glory; watch all the living saints being changed and all going up to meet the Lord in the air. I would say, 'There it is. That is what I have been telling you about. There is the Church which is His Body. There is His Flock. There is His Temple, His House. There is His Bride. There is the Mystery. Look at it going up to meet the Lord in the air; to the Marriage Supper; to the Judgment Seat of Christ!' That will be the only time on Earth that we will see the Church complete. What a beautiful story.

Church Principles for Today

When God takes us Home, He is going to present us to His Father. 'Father, My Temple! Father, here is My House!' Present us? Yes, of course, He is going to present us! Imagine you being presented to God. The Lord Jesus Christ is going to make sure that, that Bride of His has neither spot, nor wrinkle, nor any such thing, when she gets to Heaven.

My wife and I were married a long time ago. Oh, I remember it distinctly. Of course I do. How could I forget it? When we were married we had a picture taken: There I was and my young bride was beside me, over here on my right was my sister, Isobel, and over there on my bride's left-hand side, her brother, William. Twenty-five years later we had another photograph taken. We stood in the same order as we did those twenty-five years before. In my picture-album, at home, I have the picture of the day of my wedding, and there is that other, of twenty-five years later. 'Oh', you may say, 'What a change has been wrought in you, Mr. Jennings. Why, your hair used to be black and now it is grey. You used to have a full head of hair but now it is thinning'. But what about my bride? Has anything happened to her? Well, the years have had their toll on her also. You only have to compare the two to see it.

The Church and the Churches

The Lord Jesus Christ says, 'When I show you My Bride, she will not have a spot, nor wrinkle, or any such thing', for the Book of the Revelation, shows that after one thousand years of married life, she will still have the spotless beauty of the days of her espousal. Presented to God, in all her beauty.

(Incidentally, there is no such thing as members of a Church in the Bible. Members of the Body – yes. But never members of a Church, anywhere.

Further, there is no reference anywhere in the Scriptures to a, 'Church of Rome'. "The Church of the Thessalonians" – yes. "The Churches of Galatia" – yes. "The Church of God which is at Corinth" – yes. But never the Church of Rome. Perhaps God had a reason for this?)

The Churches – the similarities

Now we come to another study. God never intended that a man, or a woman, should be saved in order to live a hermit's life. That was never His plan. God determined, from the very beginning, that people, who were saved, should gather into little groups, all over the world. He never intended that they

Church Principles for Today

should live alone, to be a little entity unto themselves, living on some desert island, or in some monastery, seeking to live a holy life for Him.

God intended that these individual members of His Body should gather together into little groups, wherever it was convenient, but He expects each group to be exact replicas of that great company of people. I am going to explain the reason for that although it would take an other chapter.

I went to learn German once. I needed to follow a course in some university, or other, so I had to learn a foreign language, within one year. I had never studied a language in my life, but I needed to learn sufficient to get through this examination and I had a task before me which was going to be very difficult. So instead of going to the ordinary classes in the local college, I thought I would get a German national and pay him to teach me privately. So I did.

"Sir, will you teach me German?"

"I will."

"Good. One year is all you have, Sir, to put me through this

The Church and the Churches

examination."

He said, "All right then, I will put you through the examination if you do what I tell you."

One of the very first things he said to me was,

"Sir, if you could speak English, I could teach you German much more easily."

Now that reduced any pride I might have had!

Then he said to me, "You know, your language is not an exact language, it is not scientific. It is a careless language. Haphazard. But German is different. It is scientific. For instance, you would hold up your hand and say, 'That is my hand'. We, Germans, would not. You would point to your ear and say, 'This is my ear', but we would not".

Then he reasoned, "If I were to cut your hand off, then cut your arm off, then cut your head off, eventually, we would have you all cut off! Then where would you be?"

I did not know where I would be, if you did all that with my poor body. I could not tell him.

He said, "German is different. When we talk about parts of the body, we say, pointing to the hand, 'This is me'; or pointing to the ear, 'This is me'; or pointing to thumb, 'This is me', and so on."

All the time he was talking to me about German, I was thinking about I Corinthians, chapter 12. Because what I could see perfectly clearly was that each local representation of the whole Body of Christ, the local gathering of believers, could sincerely say, "This is me, 'The Church'". It is not a part of it. It is not a bit of it. It is not a little increment of it, but it is 'The Church'! If you look at me, I can say, "Here I am, the Church! Not a bit of it."

What God expects then, does He not, is that this little group of persons, who have gathered together, should be the exact replica of that great Church which is His Body?

That is why, in I Corinthians, chapter 12, He calls the little, local company, "My Body". Mind you, if you were to read

The Church and the Churches

verses 12 and 13, very carefully, He not only calls it, 'the Body', but look at Whose Name is applied to it. Read it and think of the majesty of what God thinks of the Local Assembly.

It is the only place in the Bible where the Lord actually calls the Assembly, 'the Assembly of Christ'. God takes I Corinthians, chapter 12 and says, 'Do you not know that you are Body of Christ.' That means there should be no schism. That means that all the members of this Assembly should work in harmony together, does it not? And does that not also mean that no one in the Assembly should say, "I am in the House, but you are not!"? That would be like me standing at the lathe, or the bench, with my one leg up. We need all the members.

Sometime ago, I fell in the snow and hurt my shoulder. Sometimes it is still a bit sore and I cannot use my arm. I try to comb my hair but I cannot. I need my other arm to reach to the top of my head. I miss my arm so badly. Some people tell me that if you loose your big toe, you would find it very difficult to balance. You might not know that you need all these members, but you do. You see, they are all working together, oiled to perfection. God wants the Body, to work in perfect harmony.

Why else does He call it a Body? Because through it He is

going to express Himself. Through it He is going to teach angels. Just as the Universal Church is to grow, so also is the Local Church to grow, from little babes, through young men, into adults. Why? Because through the members of the Assembly, He is not only going to rule in that coming Millennial Kingdom but He is going to delegate His authority to its members. That is what God thinks of the Local Assembly.

So, the very word that God gives to the Universal Church, is the very same word which He gives to the Local Church.

I am not surprised at all, when I turn to the Acts of the Apostles, chapter 20. Do you know what He calls the little Church there? 'The Flock'. Paul, the apostle, gathers the saints together in that chapter and says, 'Now you watch yourselves, brethren, won't you. You brethren who have taken the responsibility of the little Flock, for whom Christ died. Take care, you overseers, how you look after your Flock.' Oh no, He does not! That Flock, in the Acts of the Apostles, chapter 20, or in I Peter, chapter 5, or wherever you go in Scripture, is never the Flock of the overseers. Whose Flock is it then? It says, 'Watch that you take care of My Flock'. It is His! The only government who owns the sheep, is Christ. 'You behave yourselves, you shep-

The Church and the Churches

herds, and watch the way you look after My Flock'.

It is the Lord's property. He calls it by the very same name as given to that great company of people. Do you know why He calls it that? Because He loves you. He died for you and He cares and tends you every day that you live.

Would you be surprised if I told you that in I Corinthians, chapter 3, He calls the Local Church, 'His Temple'? What God calls that Universal Church, in Ephesians, chapter 2, He calls the little Assembly by the very same name. That shows me that you must never refer to the Local Assembly as part of the Temple. It **is** the Temple, the Temple of God. Do you know why? Because He dwells there. When the saints gather together, He is there in the midst. That is why we should behave ourselves. Remember that the King of Kings is in the midst of His Temple.

It is a very sad thing, in the context of I Corinthians, chapter 3, that the Lord Jesus has to say, 'He who destroys my Temple, him I will similarly destroy' (The word 'destroy' means in this instance to 'defile'). God expects the small, local Temple to be altogether holy.

Church Principles for Today

I tell you, if we were to study that portion of Scripture we would watch very carefully what we do in the Assembly. It is a tremendous responsibility for any soul to come into the Assembly of God, because it is His Temple and He wants it to be holy. Indeed, He demands it to be holy.

In many of the Assemblies in Belfast, we have a separated row of seats in the back of the Hall. My wife and I sat on those seats for a number of years. Then, after we were married, we both wanted to be brought into the fellowship of the meeting. So, the day came when my wife and I were brought in and were given our seats in the Temple.

Oh, I was in this 'Big Temple' the day I was saved, but I was not in this 'Small Temple' until the day I passed that imaginary demarcation line, of the double seat. Do you know what I thought? I thought when I passed those double seats that I was going onto holy ground. Well, was not I? Yes, of course, I was.

Oh, may God give you, and give me, the grace to remember that the small local gathering, the little Assembly in your locality, is God's Temple and He demands that it is holy.

The Church and the Churches

The Lord wants to come down and with quietness, and peace, dwell amongst a holy people. You will not bring sin into the meeting, will you? The very word by which God has called that great company of people, He also uses for the little company: His Temple.

Well, if God has called this Local Church, a Temple, tell me, what do you think He might also call it by? Well, does he call it a House? Of course, He calls it a House! He does that at the end of I Timothy, chapter 3.

He calls it that because we ought to know how we should behave ourselves in, 'the House, which is the pillar and ground of truth'. It is the Lord that reigns, not the brethren. The House has always got to do with governmental dealings.

Would it not be a wonderful thing to study discipline in the House of God? We will do that in chapter 7, and we will find that if we do not discipline ourselves, it will not be long until we find One who will, because He is Lord of His House.

We will learn that if the overseeing brethren do not govern

Church Principles for Today

the House, God will govern them and the House. It is a very, very serious thing to be a governor in the House of God. For the writer of the Epistle to the Hebrews says, 'They watch for your souls as they that must give an account'. Why young men clamour for overseership is more than I can tell. If we could catch a glimpse of the Judgement Seat of Christ and see those poor overseers, who did not have the proper qualifications, and who let all kinds of things slip into the meetings, they will wish, perhaps, that they had never become an overseer. God calls the Local Church, My House, because He is going to govern it.

Are you surprised that in the Book of the Revelation, chapter 1, He calls the little Assembly, 'A Mystery'? Is that not an amazing thing? Something that is altogether new. Something which He had hidden, in His heart, throughout those Old Testament times. Something which the angels knew nothing about. Something which was bound in the heart of God. And the name that was given to that great, vast Church, God gives to the small, Local Church: A Mystery.

In II Corinthians, chapter 11, do you know what else God

The Church and the Churches

calls the little Assembly? Says Paul, the Apostle, 'I am longing for that day when I shall present you to Him as a chaste virgin'. No corruption there. No impurity there. The desire of Paul was that the, 'little thing', should be presented, one day, to the Person of the Lord Jesus Christ, as a Bride in all her beauty and purity.

Can you not see what the Local Assembly should be? There is no end to it. But is it not clear that every single name that God uses for the Church, which is His Body, He uses for the little Local Assembly? So whatever that word, 'Body' means, whatever the word, 'Flock' means, whatever 'Temple, House, Mystery or Bride' mean, whatever those similes, or metaphors, (whichever the case might be) mean, they are intended to teach us something concerning the Church and the Churches.

We can see, therefore, the importance which God gives to His local representation. See Table 2.3.

I hope and trust God, that the Churches scattered all over the globe, show out all these characteristics of unity, care, holiness, justice, wonder and purity.

Church Principles for Today

The Cities of Refuge

Let us take a look, briefly at Joshua, chapter 20. Now, I am not saying that this is the interpretation. I am only going to take

The Church	The Churches
Body	Body (I Cor., 12)
Flock	Flock (Acts, 20)
Temple	Temple (I Cor., 3)
House	House (I Tim., 3)
Mystery	Mystery (Rev., 1)
Bride	Bride (I Cor., 11)

Table 2.3: **Various Names for the Local Church**

one or two things, from that chapter, to emphasise what I have, thus far, taught.

Joshua said, 'I want you to form cities of Refuge and I want you to call one of them Kedesh.' What does Kadesh mean? It means Sanctuary, or holiness. Could I put that along with Temple?.

The Church and the Churches

'Not only appoint Kedesh, but appoint Shechem.' What does Shechem mean? The meaning of that word is, Shoulder or government; for example, 'On His shoulder shall the government of the nations be.' Would that not go along with House?

He said, 'Thou shalt appoint Hebron.' What does Hebron mean? It means, a Joining, no schisms surely, that is similar to the Body.

'After Hebron you shall appoint another city, which is called Bezer'. What does Bezer mean? The word means, Defence. Is that not exactly what the Shepherd does to His Flock?

'I shall appoint another city and shall call it Ramoth.' What does Ramoth mean? Heights, or joy. Now, that fits the meaning of Bride.

'And thou shalt appoint even another city and shall call it Golan,' and it means Exile, a calling out. Is that not the meaning of Church? See Table 2.4.

Now, each city stood on its own base and the government of

one city had nothing to do with the government of another. Would you be surprised if I told you that the strength of the Local Church lies in this fact, that there is no central government? Let us keep it that way!

There is no Fellowship in Ireland, or England, or Wales, or Scotland, or anywhere else in the World, that has any right of

The Church	The Churches	The Cities of Refuge
Body Flock Temple House Mystery Bride		Hebron Bezer Kadesh Schechem Golan Ramoth

Table 2.4: **An Application of the Cities of Refuge**

control, in any way, over the other. There is no evangelist, or teacher, no matter who he might be, or who he might set himself up to be, has the slightest authority to come and tell the government of a meeting how to behave itself. That is not his business.

The Church and the Churches

If you have a problem that you cannot solve, then, send for a teacher to explain some passage, then send him home and think it out yourselves. There is no man who has any right to tell you what to do. The government stands on its own and is responsible to God for its outreach, unity, government, holiness and care. No one may interfere.

Is your Church like that? We find that in every one of these cities there were, what they called, elders. So, in every Local Assembly there are elders. Sometimes we call them overseers, shepherds, bishops, pastors and sometimes we call them a whole lot of other things! Those shepherds are responsible to God for the Assembly, which they govern. What a wonderful thing.

The Door into the Local Church

I was saved on the 21st. May, 1935, and was gathered to the Name of the Lord Jesus Christ, on 17th. September 1944. I have not been able to get to all the meetings in all those years, but I have been to a good number and I must honestly confess that I have never yet heard any of my beloved brethren telling how somebody can get into the Local Assembly. In a word, what is the Scriptural method of reception? I would like to deal with that in as gentle a way as I can.

Sometimes, when teaching, we use illustrations because it helps others to understand. The Lord Jesus did that, Paul did it also, and James is full of it. So, there is no harm in going to the Old Testament Scriptures, if you wish, to use them as illustrations. So, having laid the above foundation, let us deal with the reception into this Local Church.

Somebody asks, "Is everybody on this Earth in this Universal Church?"

"No!"

"How do you get into it?"

"By one simple word: Obedience."

But someone else might say, "I thought you got in by believing." Believing is obedience, is not it? Do you not read, in the New Testament, of those that obeyed not Gospel? Is that not what it says? Does Hebrews, chapter 4, not tell us that belief and obedience is one and the same word? On the very day that you came to trust in the Lord Jesus Christ as your Saviour, you

The Church and the Churches

were simply being obedient. The Lord Jesus said, "Come unto me", and what did you do? You obeyed! That is how you were saved.

We are told, 'If thou wilt confess with thy mouth Jesus as thy Lord'.

"Oh yes, I will. I will obey."

I did that on the 21st of May, 1935.

Obedience. Obedience to what? Obedience to the Person of the Lord Jesus Christ. When I obeyed the Chief Shepherd, in that instant I became part of the Universal Church.

Tell me, are you saved? I am saved. Are you in the Local Church. Not yet. Do you mean to tell me you can be in one and not in the other? Yes. There are hundreds, and thousands, of saints that are saved and are not yet in that local gathering. Indeed, many, many souls have been in the local gathering and later found that they had never been saved! It is possible to be in one but not in the other; possible to be in the Local Church but not in the Universal Church. It is possible to be in neither. It is possible to be in both.

Church Principles for Today

How did I get into the Universal Church? Obedience to the Chief Shepherd. How do you get into the Local Church? Reams could be written on that. Can I put it to you in a word? The Lord Jesus said, 'I am the Chief Shepherd and what I am going to do is to take shepherds, not one, many; I am going to take shepherds and put those shepherds in charge of this little Flock'. One Shepherd for the Universal Church, but a plurality of shepherds for the Local Church. The day is coming when those shepherds shall stand before the Chief Shepherd and give an account to Him of the way they looked after the sheep of His pasture.

How can I get into the Local Church? In a word, how do you become a member of the church? By obedience! You cannot let Tom, Dick and Harry in. Well, you can if they are all saved, and if they are all agreeing to be obedient to what the demands are, in the Local Assembly.

I want to tell you, that at the very instant that you believed in the Person of the Lord Jesus Christ, you were Baptised into the Spirit of God, by Christ.

There is no such thing as a soul being in the Universal

The Church and the Churches

Church without being Baptised into the Spirit of God. Should everybody be baptised who is in the Local Church? Of course, they should be baptised. That is a demand. Is it not the shepherds' responsibility to see that all those that are in the little Flock are baptised and obedient to the commandments of the Lord? Now, there are circumstances, I know, when people are very, very ill, and they dare not go under the water. God understands all these things. But nevertheless the New Testament Scripture does not visualise anybody who is part of the Local Church and not baptised. It is the shepherds' job to see that they are.

"Are you baptised, son?"

"Not yet."

"Well, you have to be baptised."

"What do I do until I learn it?"

"Why not just come and let us see how you behave yourself. If you like, occupy the 'seat of the unlearned'".

"How dare you say I am unlearned".

Now, do you not want to hear, and learn, about obedience to the government? God does not want any schism in His House. He wants that House to be governed and the government of the House demands, 'Go and baptise'. Therefore, no one is accepted into the Local House, unless baptised, except in extreme cases, when God understands.

One day a dear soul came to the gate of the city, but he did not come in. He saw the elders, at the gate, and asked,

"May I come in?"

"What is your story?" They asked.

You would not object to telling the overseers your story, would you?

"When did you get saved, son? How did you get saved, son?"

Do not be afraid. Do not think they are trying to make little of you. They are only guarding the House. They have the responsibility to look after these things. They just cannot let anybody in. You do not want somebody in that is going to wreck the fellowship, do you? They are going to have to give an account for you, in a coming day. The young man came to the elders of the city and told his story, and they studied it. Sometimes they let him in, but sometimes they kept him out.

Do you know, that I was kept out for a long time? Do you

The Church and the Churches

know what I did? I went home in a huff! No, I did not! I just sat at the back until eventually, I was allowed in.

Do not be upset if the government, of the Local Church, do not let you in immediately. Do not be upset if they say, "Wait a little while". The way I looked at it was, if the Lord comes, He will know that I wanted in, He will know that I asked and they will have to tell God why they did not let me in. I was quite content to sit at the back. What a dreadful thing if they let someone in who would destroy the meeting. What a disaster if they kept somebody out who should have been in! Would you like to be an overseer? Think twice about it.

Now that the believer is in, what did the government do? They gave him a place! They gave him something to do. They let him feel that he was part of the Temple, the House ... they let him feel he was part and not somebody on the outskirts.

Is it not lovely that when you are brought into the meeting, the love is extended?

"Can you teach in the Sunday School, sister? Could you give

out books at the door, son?"

They gave him a place. Oh, the sisters have places too. Do not be too upset, if the government of the meeting tells you that, in God's wisdom, the beloved sisters have different roles to men. They are only doing their best to be obedient to God's commands. That is all. We will deal with this, in chapter 8.

Obedience is the way you get in.

How long did they stay in the city of refuge? It tells you how long. They stayed inside the city until the High Priest died. I tell you, that will be a long time, as far as I am concerned, because I have a High Priest who liveth to perpetuity. If I am going to stay in the Local Assembly until my High Priest dies, then I am going to be here a long time!

The Churches – the differences

I have shown you how alike the Local Church ought to be with the Universal Church. Now, what I want to do is to show you how very different we really are.

Here is the first point! Do you know who builds that Univer-

The Church and the Churches

sal Church? Yes, of course. It is the Gospel preacher. He stands up and does his best to preach the Gospel of the grace of the Lord Jesus. It is also all the brethren, and sisters, who pray. Then, before the meeting is over, one here, and one there, is saved. What a wonderful preacher he is! Do you know what he did? He added ten people to the Church, which is His Body. He did no such thing! There is only one Person who adds to the Church, which is His Body. Only One. That is Christ. He adds to the Body, or to the Church, such that should be saved. It is not given to you, or to me, or to any other soul on this wide Earth, to save one single solitary man or woman. We found that out, in chapter 1.

I remember well the day when I could have used one thumb to point out all the persons that ever were saved through my ministry. Then, happy day, I needed a finger; happy day when I needed a hand; happy, happy day when I needed two. But that would do me. What a grand fellow I am! Ten people have been saved through me. I never saved one of them! The Lord Jesus used me as a channel of blessing but it was He who did the saving. That is why we pray; that is why we study the Scriptures, because we know that no man, on Earth, can extend the Kingdom of Christ. Christ builds and He alone. That is why it is perfect.

Church Principles for Today

Tell me, who builds the Local Church? Oh, I Corinthians, chapter 3, says, 'You brethren, watch how you build'. Is there a possibility that some of us are building a lot of straw? Perhaps, some are building a pile of wood? At the Judgment Seat of Christ, wooooof! The whole lot gone in flames. Oh, how men can destroy things! Or will you be found at the Judgment Seat of Christ, having builded those jewels, or gold, or silver?

Can you see in the Universal Church, that it is Christ who is building? Can you see in the Local Church that it is men who are building? That is why, at times, we hear and see all sorts of strange things. Do we not? That is why, sometimes, sadness, and division, and strife come into the Local Church – because God has put the responsibility of it upon us to build.

Then we read, "There is therefore now no condemnation to them which are in Christ Jesus, who walk not after the flesh, but after the Spirit." Who are these people? They are members of that vast, vast Assembly of believing Christians. It would be easy for me to prove that, from the Epistle to the Hebrews, chapters 8 and 10. Your sins past, present and future were put away, the moment you trusted Christ. Your eternal salvation is utterly and absolutely secure and once saved you can never,

The Church and the Churches

never be lost. There is no condemnation. There is no cloud between you and God. Not one.

Indeed should you die without confession of sins you would be, 'Absent from the body and present with the Lord'. You say, "I would love to find where you get that". I have already quoted to you, Romans, chapter 8, verse 1. I can also quote, I Corinthians, chapter 15, where I find that when He comes, we will be taken up to be with Him in the air. Who, Lord? Those that are asleep and those that are awake. Who are those that are asleep? The dead? No, no! Read the context of the passage. Those that are living near to Him and those, who are saved, but are living away from Him. So, in the Church, which is His Body, there is no condemnation. None at all. Sins past, present and future are all put away – altogether and absolutely.

What about the Local Church? Can the brethren say, "No condemnation"? I should think not. What does I Corinthians, chapter 5, say, 'Put away from yourselves that wicked person'. What has happened now? Judgment. That man, in I Corinthians, chapter 5, is put outside the Assembly because he has been judged! What about his salvation? Ah, that is all right! "That the spirit may be saved in the day of the Lord Jesus." Still saved!

Church Principles for Today

However, the Lord Jesus Christ also said, "I will build my church". Look at it. "I will build my church and the gates of Hell shall not prevail against it", and all the power of hell could not rob God of one single solitary soul. Not one! Evil cannot prevail against it. Are you listening? Can the power of Hell prevail against the Local Assembly? Oh, yes! Oh, yes it can. Do you know what the devil can do? Within a space of a few months he could close the door. Oh, yes, he could.

When I went to Manchester, in 1964, I got a map and I put an 'X' where I had to stay. I got the address of every Assembly in the city and put other 'X's' to represent them in their various localities. I looked to see which was the nearest to me and that is where I went. It just so happened that it was one of the most prosperous Assemblies in Manchester. The conferences were held there. They had a cellar as big as the hall, a gallery at the back and a gallery at the front. Oh what a place. Crammed, full with people.

A couple of years later one of the brethren rang me up and he said, "Brother Rowan, I have sad news. The doors are locked." It was not trouble from without and that is all I am going to tell you. That is all he told me and that is all I know.

The Church and the Churches

Sometime later, I was in Manchester and I was passing Ardwood Green on the bus, and I took a look at the old hall. I could hardly keep the tears from streaming down my cheek, as I looked over at it. It was some canteen or other. That is where the brethren used to preach! The gates of Hell shall not prevail against the Church, which is His Body, but the gates of Hell had prevailed against Ardwood Green Gospel Hall, and that great Assembly's doors were closed and will never be opened again.

It would not take the devil long to close the Assembly's doors where you attend. It could not happen in Northern Ireland! Could it not? Oh, yes it could, and it has. A few years ago, I could have taken you to a door and shown you a great big lock on it because no one was allowed to enter.

Just after the war years I was in the Republic of Ireland. The man who was with me asked,

"Do you see that wee hall?"

I said "Yes, I do indeed."

He said, "That used to be a lovely little Assembly, but not now."

Church Principles for Today

It was not the government that closed its doors. It was not the National Church that closed its doors. It was not violence, nor persecution. It came from within, and the doors were shut. Would it not be an awful thing if the Assembly to which you belong, dear reader, would one day be shut and you would be able to look back and say, "I did not take the advice. I allowed the devil to prevail against us"?

Oh, indeed, there is a difference between the Church and the Churches. Would you let me look at just two more?

What is this I see over this great Flock of God? I see a great canopy of love over it. Did anyone ever love it like Him? There is not a pain you have, but He understands. He tends you, watches you and cares for you. He has you on His shoulder, no, on His shoulders, He will never let you down until He gets you Home.

What about the little Assembly? In charge of it there are under-shepherds, are there not? Those men who take their cue from the Chief Shepherd. They tend, and watch, and love, and care, and feed, and guide the Flock as He does. They do - do they not? Then, one day, they shall stand, says I Peter, chapter

The Church and the Churches

5, before the Great Shepherd of the sheep and receive rewards, as only shepherds can receive, according to how they have cared for us.

Finally, do you know how long this great Church is going to last? For ever, and ever! It is eternal in its duration.

How long is the Local Assembly going to last? At the longest, "Till He come". We do not know just how soon He may come, but when He comes, that will be the end of the Local Witness. Indeed, it could end sooner than that, as I said, because the devil might close the doors, if you do not watch.

I suppose we would have to do an awful lot of evil things for the devil to close the door. Do you know what the Lord Jesus said in the Book of the Revelation, chapter 3? He said, 'If you do not go back to your first love, I will remove your candlestick.' It is just as simple as that.

There is no end to these comparisons. Oh, how alike we should be, but sadly, how different we really are!

Chapter 3

The Baptism in the Spirit

Our first reading, for this chapter, is to be found in:

The Epistle of Paul the Apostle to the Ephesians, chapter 1, verses 20 - 23:

"Which he wrought in Christ, when he raised him from the dead, and set him at his own right hand in the heavenly places, Far above all principality, and power, and might, and dominion, and every name that is named, not only in this world, but also in that which is to come: And hath put all things under his

Church Principles for Today

feet, and gave him to be the head over all things to the Church, Which is his body, the fullness of him that filleth all in all."

Then, in Ephesians, chapter 2, verses 6 - 8a:

"And hath raised us up together, and made us sit together in heavenly places in Christ Jesus: That in the ages to come he might shew the exceeding riches of his grace in his kindness toward us through Christ Jesus. For by grace are ye saved ...."

Then, also, in Ephesians, chapter 3, verses 9 - 10:

"And to make all men see what is the fellowship of the mystery, which from the beginning of the world hath been hid in God, who created all things by Jesus Christ: To the intent that now unto the principalities and powers in heavenly places might be known by the Church the manifold wisdom of God."

And in Ephesians, chapter 4, verses 11 - 13:

"And he gave some, apostles; and some, prophets; and some, evangelists; and some, pastors and teachers; For the perfecting of the saints, for the work of the ministry, for the edifying of the body of Christ: Till we all come in the unity of the

The Baptism in the Spirit

faith, and of the knowledge of the Son of God, unto a perfect man, unto the measure of the stature of the fullness of Christ:"

And finally, in Revelation, chapter 1, verses 18-20:

"I am he that liveth, and was dead; and, behold, I am alive for evermore, Amen; and have the keys of hell and of death. Write the things which thou hast seen, and the things which are, and the things which shall be hereafter; The mystery of the seven stars which thou sawest in my right hand, and the seven golden candlesticks. The seven stars are the angels of the seven Churches: and the seven candlesticks which thou sawest are the seven Churches.

The Introduction

The first part of the reading, for this chapter, might sound a little academic, however, I want to assure you, from my wanderings around the Assemblies, not only in Belfast, but further afield, that what I am going to set before you, is an essential feature of our Church gatherings, which is not always readily appreciated

Church Principles for Today

New Testament Baptisms

What I want to talk about is called the, "Baptism in the Spirit". This great subject is generally misunderstood and yet our Assemblies would be guarded against the inroads of many queer doctrines, if all the saints understood exactly what is meant by this "Baptism in the Spirit".

We read of this Spirit Baptism, in Matthew, chapter 3. We read of it again, in Mark, chapter 1. We read of it again, in Luke, chapter 3. Then again, in John, chapter 1. When we come to the Acts of the Apostles, we find it in chapter 1, then again in chapter 11, and those are the only places, in the whole of the Acts of the Apostles, where it is to be found. Finally, I Corinthians, chapter 12, is the only reference in all the epistles where Baptism of the Spirit is referred to.

If we were to take all these seven passages and look at them very carefully, we would find, without any difficulty, some very important facts.

One of the things we see, on the very surface of all these passages, is that there are four facets to be found in all Baptisms.

The Baptism in the Spirit

(You may not know what a facet is, but do not worry. You will understand it perfectly as you continue reading.)

You will find, if you study Matthew, Mark, Luke, John and those two passages in Acts, that there is always a person who does the baptising. I can remember, very well, the night that I was baptized in the tank in Windsor Gospel Hall, Belfast. The man who baptized me was a Mr. Madill. But what is true of Baptism in water is similarly true of this Baptism in the Spirit. So the first thing we notice is, that in any Baptism, there is always the person who does the baptising. Now that seems so elementary, that it is hardly worth telling you. Elementary as it might seem, however, it is vitally important when we come to the Baptism into the Holy Spirit.

Then again, it will hardly be worth mentioning that there is always the person who is baptized. Again, I remember the night I was baptized. While it is true that Mr. Madill was the one who did the baptizing, yet I was the person who was being baptized. We will see before the end of this chapter, that in Spirit Baptism this fact is also applicable.

Firstly, there must be a person who does the baptizing and,

secondly, there must be the person who is baptized. So elementary that it is hardly worth mentioning.

Then thirdly, there must always be an element in which the Baptism takes place. You must be baptized into something. When I was baptized, the element into which I was baptized, the thing, the stuff, was water.

One time I was asked to baptize some people, away in the wilds of the country, where they had a tank which was nearly as porous as a sieve. There was one very large man and two others to be baptized. When I saw the man, I said to the dear saints, "Will you fill the tank well up with water?" So they did. They filled it with buckets. By the time I had given a word of ministry, however, the water had nearly all drained away! I was left with a drop of water, well, about two feet at the bottom of the tank, in which to baptize this great man. You know, the two of us nearly got baptized! I wanted plenty of water so that the man's buoyancy would help raise him but because there was only a little water left, I almost lost my balance, which was exactly what I thought I would do. It was only by a stroke of ingenuity that I got him out of the water. But what I wanted, and managed, to do was to get the man right down into the water

The Baptism in the Spirit

and out of it again. The element in which the Baptism took place, was water.

But there is a fourth point, which is of vital importance. There is not only the person who does the baptizing; there is not only the person who is baptized; there is not only the element in which the person is baptized, but there is always a purpose. Why were you baptized? What was your reason? We will discuss this in greater detail with regards to water Baptism, in chapter 5.

When we study these four points, we must try to apply them to every Baptism that is mentioned in the New Testament Scriptures.

Let us try to apply these, for example, to John's Baptism. It tells us, perfectly plainly, that John was baptizing. So we can see, first of all, who did the actual baptizing. How exceedingly simple! There is not one who could have any difficulty there.

When we read the Scriptures again, we find out who John baptized and it is also very simple. Jews came and were baptized. So John was the baptizer and persons, human beings, were being baptized.

Then we find, without any difficulty at all, sitting right on the very surface, that John baptized in water. It says so.

Now, we are absolutely indebted to dear Matthew, for in chapter 3 and verse 11, he says, "...unto repentance." There is the purpose. Without Matthew we would not have known the purpose, the reason, for John's Baptism.

I am not going to explain to you John's Baptism. I only took that particular illustration to point out these four facets of Baptisms, generally.

Baptism in the Spirit

What I want to do is to study these four facets, as they are applied to this Spirit Baptism.

When we come to Spirit Baptism we would find, in the above mentioned Scriptures, that John the Baptist said, 'Even as I baptize, so there is One coming, a greater than I, who also

The Baptism in the Spirit

shall baptize'. This Baptism of which John spoke is the Baptism in the Spirit, and it is of vital importance to us.

First of all, we would find that John the Baptist said perfectly clearly, 'There cometh One after me Who shall baptize'. Now is that not clear? We all know Who the One was, Who was greater than John. John's Gospel, chapter 1, makes that perfectly clear. The Lord Jesus Christ was going to do the baptizing. That could not be clearer and yet it is paramount to what I want to say, because today many people are running around looking for the, "Baptism of the Spirit" - as if it was the Spirit who did the baptizing. The Spirit does not do the baptizing, it is Christ who does it. So the first point is vital, if we are to understand Spirit Baptism correctly - it is the Lord Jesus Christ who does the baptizing.

The second point is, who does Christ baptize? I want to stress, to you, that He baptizes only believers. Not sinners, but believers. So just as John was the baptizer and baptized human beings, who were Jews, so the Lord Jesus Christ is the baptizer and He baptizes human beings also, but who are saved.

The third point is regarding the element of this Baptism. Not only does the Lord Jesus baptize but He baptizes into an element, and that element is the Holy Spirit. So instead of the Holy Spirit being the baptizer, as some argue, the One who does the baptizing is Christ and the element into which the believer is baptized is the Spirit.

Now, that is not easy to grasp, I am not one bit surprised that John said, 'There cometh a Greater after me.' A greater than John? How much greater? Well, I have baptized people, dozens of them. It was not an impossible thing for me to take a person and baptize them in water. However, to baptize a person into the Holy Spirit of God is something that no man on Earth can do. That is something that only Christ can do.

The fourth facet of this Baptism in the Holy Spirit is the reason, or purpose, for it. This is not given in Matthew, nor Mark, nor Luke, nor John, nor Acts, but it is given to us in I Corinthians, chapter 12. The purpose for this Baptism is that we might all become, 'one Body'. That is not so easy to understand. It seems a bit academic. But I am going to try and make it as clear as I can, because it is most important.

Now, are you reading this carefully? I am going to prove a

The Baptism in the Spirit

difference between the coming of the Holy Spirit and this Baptism in the Holy Spirit. That may sound strange to you, especially those who are theologians! I am saying, categorically, that the coming of the Holy Spirit, in Acts, chapter 2, happened once and once only. It never had happened before, and it has never happened since. But the Baptism in the Spirit is an entirely different thing. Let me show you what I mean.

If we were to study Acts, chapter 2 for a moment, we would find that after the Lord Jesus Christ had gone Home, to Heaven, those dear brethren and sisters, in Christ, went back to Jerusalem, to an upper room, and there they waited until the 'Day of Pentecost was fully come'. Suddenly, on that day, the whole room was filled with a noise of this rushing mighty wind – the Holy Spirit of God had come down from Heaven. The Holy Spirit had come, to dwell on Earth.

But, the very first time this Baptism in the Holy Spirit took place was in Acts of the Apostles, chapter 2, verses 2 - 4. It reads like this: And suddenly there came a sound from heaven as of a rushing mighty wind, and it filled all the house where they were sitting. And there appeared unto them cloven tongues like as of fire, and it sat upon each of them. *And they were all filled with the Holy Ghost.* That was when Christ first baptized into the Holy Spirit.

We saw in chapter 2, God saved this company of people, and baptized them by Christ, into the Holy Spirit, in order to call them, 'a Body'.

Thus, we find two things happened on that remarkable day: Firstly, the Holy Spirit of God took up His abode on Earth and, secondly, the believers were baptised into Him.

When we come to the Gospel according to John, chapter 4, we find that, 'The Jews have no dealings with Samaritans'. One day the Lord Jesus Christ was on a journey and He sat by a well and a dear woman came along, who was a Samaritan. He began to talk to her and when His disciples came along, they marvelled, that the Lord Jesus should condescend to speak to a Samaritan. Why? Because, 'The Jews have no dealings with the Samaritans'.

If, in Acts, chapter 2, the Jews have been brought into this

The Baptism in the Spirit

thing called, 'the Body', they certainly would not have Samaritans in it! The unbelieving Jews would sneer and say, 'This is a new sect that we have'.

Is it not a marvellous thing what God has done? For in the Acts of the Apostles, chapter 8, there are a number of Samaritans, the very people with whom the Jews would have no dealings at all, and they hear the Gospel. Not only that, but they believe it and are baptized with water, but the Scripture distinctly says that they did not receive the Holy Spirit. Why? If God is going to prove that this Church, this Body, that He is forming, is going to include Jews and Samaritans, He is going to have to convince those Jews to accept the Samaritans.

When the Jewish brethren, of Jerusalem, heard about salvation coming to the Samaritans, they immediately sent James and John down to investigate. While these, most important of Jewish witnesses, were there, the Spirit of God fell on the Samaritans. He did not have to come down again to do this because He was already here. He had already taken up His abode, here on Earth. James and John must have been shocked! Samaritans? Is it possible that God is going to include in this Body, not only Jews but also Samaritans? The Jews certainly got their eyes opened that day! God actually showed them by the Baptism in the Holy Spirit, on these particular Samaritans, that they must also be included in the Body.

We read that there is another class of people and the Jews will have absolutely no dealings with them either. They are the Gentiles.

Then a most amazing thing happened. In Acts, chapter 10, there was a Gentile, called Cornelius, a most devout and wonderful man. One day, the Holy Spirit came to Peter and told him to go down and preach to him. He did, but do you know what he also did? He took six witnesses with him. As he preached the Gospel, with these witnesses standing looking on, the Gentiles believed, and immediately the Holy Spirit of God came into them.

God showed them that not only were the Samaritans to be included in this Body, but the Gentiles also. Indeed, of such vital importance was this, that God almost uses two full chapters, in the Acts of the Apostles, to show exactly how the Gentiles were accepted, if you like, by the Jews, into the Body. What an amazing thing!

The Baptism in the Spirit

No wonder it says that the Jewish people were astounded. Let me tell you: Anything less than this would not have done. The only reason why the Jews recognised Gentiles, as being in the Body, was because they had manifestly been baptized with the Holy Spirit.

Now, you know as well as I, that the Jews will have no dealings with Gentiles. Do you know what Jews actually called Gentiles? They called them, "Dogs". One day, the Lord Jesus Christ was sitting at table and a poor Gentile came, and she asked,

'Will you heal my daughter?'

And the Lord Jesus said, 'It is not right for Me to take the children's food (the Jews) and give it to dogs (to Gentiles)?"

She said, 'That is true, Lord. That would not be the right thing to do but would You object to a dog eating a few of the crumbs that fell from the masters table?'

And the Lord said, 'Now, where did I see faith like this?'

In Philippians, chapter 3, it talks about the Gentile dogs. Psalm 22, talks about the dogs around the cross. Dogs? Yes! Gentiles. Do you mean to tell me that having been a Jew all your life, you would dare to sit down with a Gentile dog, at the Lord's Supper? Would you dare to suggest to a Jew that the Spirit of God had come to take up His abode in a Gentile dog? The answer is, "No!"

If God is going to show that there are no longer Jews, nor Gentiles, but that they are all one in Christ Jesus, that God has broken down the middle wall of partition between these two, then He is going to have to work a miracle in the Gentiles, as well as the Jews. Indeed, the Spirit of God is going to have to come down on the Gentiles, exactly as He came down on the Jews, at the beginning, and it will have to be manifested in exactly the same way.

Now there is another class! I am not going to explain this in depth because it is not our subject, but it would not be hard to turn to the Acts of the Apostles, chapter 19, and find a fourth class of people on whom the Holy Spirit was to fall. They were a class of people who were saved, who had believed in the Lord Jesus, and yet had never heard of either Christian Baptism, nor of the Holy Spirit. As Paul the Apostle, in chapter 19, preached to them, the Holy Spirit fell on them - they were baptised into the Holy Spirit - and they were, therefore, also included in the

The Baptism in the Spirit

Body of Christ.

Now we come to a crucial point. Only four times, in all the Acts of the Apostles, does the Spirit of God fall on people. He fell on those Jews, in chapter 2; He fell on Samaritans, in chapter 8; He fell on Gentiles in chapter 10 and He fell on John's disciples, in chapter 19. Do you see what God is doing? He was showing that the rifts which existed between different classes of people would not, and must not, be carried into the Church, which is His Body. If there are rifts of any sort in an Assembly, or between Assemblies, or between Christians, you can rest assured that God never intended it.

Here were Jews who would have no dealings with Samaritans; here were Jews who would have no dealings with Gentiles, and here were people of an entirely different era, and if God had not worked the miracle of Baptism in the Holy Spirit, it would have led to one miniature Body of Christ for Jews, one miniature Body of Christ for Samaritans, one miniature Body of Christ for Gentiles and one miniature Body of Christ for Old Testament saints. In other words, there would have been a schism in the Body of Christ for all time. Therefore, God put an end to that before it even started. He baptized those Jews in the

Church Principles for Today

Holy Spirit, in Acts, chapter 2; He baptized those Samaritans in the Holy Spirit, in Acts, chapter 8; He baptized those Gentiles in the Holy Spirit, in Acts, chapter 10; and He baptized those Old Testament saints in the Holy Spirit, in Acts, chapter 19. There is no one outside of those four. What an amazing thing!

Then we would find another very interesting thing. How did they know they had received the Spirit? Do not think that the Baptism in the Spirit is noticed by some funny feeling up your spine? Many other things can give you funny feelings up your spine and it will not be the Holy Spirit at all.

Many a time, sometimes for little reason, at all, I feel suddenly happy. I do not know why! The doctor would tell me adrenaline, or something, has come from somewhere, or another, and gives me this feeling of happiness. It certainly does not mean that I got a new Baptism of the Holy Spirit!

Therefore, how could these people prove exclusively that they had received the Holy Spirit? The Bible will tell you. In Acts, chapter 2, no sooner had the Spirit baptized them than

The Baptism in the Spirit

they began to speak with Tongues. That was the proof! In Acts, chapter 8, when the Samaritans believed on the Lord Jesus Christ it says that Simon saw something. What did he see? Doubtlessly, he saw the manifestation of the Holy Spirit through the speaking in Tongues. In Acts of the Apostles, chapter 10, when the Holy Spirit of God baptized those Gentile believers into the Body of Christ, they spake with Tongues. There was the proof that they had received the Spirit. In Acts, chapter 19, when these disciples of John received the Spirit, they spake in Tongues.

Is it not an interesting thing that those are the only times, in the whole of the Acts of the Apostles, when there is any mention made of Tongues? It is perfectly clear, therefore, that the reason why these people spoke in Tongues was to prove, to those Jews that were round about, that they had been baptized in the Spirit.

So this great Body of Christ is going to contain Jews, Samaritans, Gentiles. Thus, there is no reason for schisms in the Body of Christ.

Church Principles for Today

No Unsaved in The Body

There is another thing which we sometimes fail to notice. In I Corinthians, chapter 12, verse 13, it not only says that we were baptized into the Spirit, at salvation, but also that we need to drink of that Spirit. That is something different, is it not? If I am baptized in water, I go into water, but if I drink water, it goes into me. Here it says, in I Corinthians, that not only did Christ baptize men into the Spirit, but He put the Spirit into them; and, says the Epistle to the Romans, it is impossible for a man to have the Spirit in him and to be unsaved. Indeed, just as this body of mine lives in air, yet air is in my body, so the very moment that these people were baptized in the Spirit, the Spirit of God entered them. They not only had the Spirit in them but they were in the Spirit.

Some may say, 'I do not see much sense in that'. Well, there are Christians today who believe that the Holy Spirit lives in them but they are not in Him. I Corinthians, chapter 12, makes it perfectly clear, that this is impossible, absolutely impossible.

Romans, chapter 8, verse 9, stresses this very point when it says, "Now if any man have not the Spirit of Christ, he is none of his." What does this mean? It means that if I have not the

The Baptism in the Spirit

Spirit of Christ, I am not saved! Notice the wording, "ye are ... in the Spirit, if so be that the Spirit of God dwell in you". I am in the Spirit, if I am saved, therefore, the Spirit must be in me. We see this double truth, then, that we cannot have one without the other. It is impossible.

So, let me tell you, clearly, that you received the Holy Spirit of God the very moment you believed. The very instant you trusted the Person of the Lord Jesus Christ, as your Saviour, the Holy Spirit took up His abode in you and at that very same instant you got baptized into the Holy Spirit. So you need not wait for His coming to you, you already have Him.

I remember well the day I was saved, I did not know anything about the Holy Spirit. Nothing at all. I had no funny feeling up my spine, nor did I see any images on the wall. I saw nothing and I felt nothing. Yet I have the audacity to tell you that on the 21st. May, 1935, Christ baptized me into the Holy Spirit and, as well, He put the Holy Spirit in me.

I did not speak in Tongues. Why? I should have, should I not? They did that in the Acts of Apostles, chapter 2, when the Spirit came upon the Jews; they did that in chapter 10, when the

Spirit of God came upon the Gentiles; they did that in chapter 19, when the Spirit of God came upon the disciples of John: So why did I not begin to speak in Tongues when I was baptized in the Spirit and the Spirit of God was given to me? Did you ever ask yourself, why Paul did not speak with Tongues the moment he was baptized in the Holy Spirit, the moment he was saved? The reason is because there was nothing else that had to be proved.

These people, in the Acts of the Apostles, had to speak in Tongues in order to prove, conclusively, to the bystanders, that the Spirit of God had come on them: Prove, conclusively, to these Jews, that the Samaritans, and the Gentiles, and the disciples of John, are all going to be made one. The only way that could be done was by allowing them to speak in Tongues.

Do I need to speak in Tongues today to prove that I have got the Holy Spirit of God? No! Why? Because this verse makes perfectly clear that, 'If I have not the Spirit of God, I am not His.' But I am His! Then I have the Spirit of God! Therefore, I do not need Tongues.

Now that is very significant, very significant indeed, and ex-

The Baptism in the Spirit

tremely necessary. If you get this into your heart and mind, you will have no trouble with the Tongues Movement. Absolutely none.

Now, I have laboured that, but it is very important because so many dear believers are going astray and are being sidetracked by strange doctrines connected with these things.

Characteristics of the Body of Christ

What I want to do now is to give you some characteristics of this Body.

In this section, I will freely interchange the use of the words, Assembly and Church. The word, "Assembly", or "Church", if you prefer, is the translation of one word in the original language it is translated some 118 times as, 'Church', in our New Testaments, whereas it is translated only three times as, 'Assembly'. Nevertheless, it is the same word.

One of those characteristics is that it represents Christ's finished work. You have no part of it, none at all. You could not save a soul. You could not even create an anxious thought in the heart of a person. That is Christ's work and His alone. I wish some of us, who preach the Gospel, would remember that. If it is God that gives the Gift of Evangelism to some beloved brother and through his ministry many souls are saved, we must ever remember, what we found in chapter 2, that the brother in question has not enlarged the Kingdom of God. You cannot enlarge God's Kingdom, only God can. It is only Christ that can take people and put them into the Body of Christ. No one else.

Then, if we look a little further, we would find that once a person comes into this Body, once he is baptized into the Spirit and the Spirit indwells him, once his sins are forgiven, once he takes the Lord Jesus Christ as Saviour, then there is no condemnation to that soul. There is not one shadow that exits between that soul and God. Thus, we have those beautiful verses in Romans, chapter 8, which we noticed in chapter 1, "Who can lay any thing to the charge of God's elect?" There is not an angel in Heaven, or a demon in Hell, that can point one finger at any one saint on Earth, because this is Christ's work and He has put away sin by the sacrifice of Himself. There is no judgment in it.

The Baptism in the Spirit

Another characteristic of this Body is that God's purpose for it is eternal. We have already shown that in the Ages to come God will use this Body for the government of His nation, for the government of His Kingdom, for the government of the coming universe. God is going to use this Body as a channel, as an instrument, of His administration. We also saw earlier, that in the Ages to come He will show His kindness through this Body. Therefore, His Body is eternal in character. When the resurrection comes it will not change. It will be the Body of Christ, forever. It can never cease to exist. Never! What a beautiful thought!

Then we would find that only saved people are in the Body. There is no unsaved person in the Body of Christ. Not one. There are no professors in the Body of Christ. No, not one. God knows very well how much sin has cost Him. But when a dear soul accepts the Lord Jesus as Saviour, with the simplicity of a child, God is satisfied. Immediately, he is baptized into the Body, immediately he becomes a possessor of the Holy Spirit of God, immediately he becomes a member of the Body of Christ. There are no professors in it, none at all.

Another wonderful thing about this Body is that once you

are in, you can never be put out. There is no Scripture in all Holy Writ to show me that having been baptized into the Body of Christ, that I can ever come out of it. There is no such thing. When Christ does a job, He does it right. When He puts me in, I am there to stay. Even though, at times, I fail; even though, at times, I do things I ought not to do (which of us does not?), there still remains no cloud between Him and me. I am in the Body of Christ. What a lovely, lovely thought.

The Lord Jesus Christ said, 'I will build My Church and the devil himself cannot prevail against it'. The devil cannot lay a finger on a member of that Church which is His Body. Feigning, he would drag us down, but he cannot touch us. We are beyond his power.

Furthermore, he cannot defile it. It is impossible. We have seen that, in a day to come, according to Ephesians, chapter 5, the Lord Jesus Christ is going to present this Body unto Himself without blemish and without spot. Even you and even me! It cannot be defiled.

The Baptism in the Spirit

Sometimes we might say, as far as the Body of Christ is concerned, we are 'in Christ'. We saw, in chapter 2, that this wonderful concept is absolutely new. It is called, 'a Mystery', in the New Testament. A Mystery is something that was altogether hidden from the saints, and patriarchs, of old. Those angels above which have been with God for thousands of years and, perhaps, felt they knew God well, stand back in utter wonder and amazement when, suddenly, there bursts a brand new plan they knew nothing about: The Body of Christ.

The Local Representation of the Body of Christ

Now we come a little bit nearer to ourselves. It was always in God's mind that the members of this Body, that happen to be in a particular place, should meet together. It was never God's intention that individual members should exist alone. It was never in God's mind that the members of this Body should just dwell in their own homes and sit at their own little corner, reading the Scriptures and praying. God's idea was that the members of His Body, in any particular district, city or country, should gather together into little groups. That was His plan.

Church Principles for Today

When we read the Book of the Revelation, chapter 1, we see that the gathering was symbolised by a candlestick or, more properly, a lampstand. So God in His grace sees a number of these members of the Church, of the Body of Christ, gather together in a town, called Ephesus. There they were, all of them, gathered together in a little group and God said, 'There is a Church.' Then over there, in the town of Pergamos, there was another group of dear believers who were also gathered together. So altogether, in the Book of the Revelation, we see seven candlesticks and it says, perfectly clearly, that each one of these is a Church.

That is exactly what God desired and that is what He desires still. He does not want us to be loners. He wants the saints to gather together and wherever the members of the Body of Christ gather, that is a Church. I wish we could understand these things. But I do not think that we do.

Now, although this is not hard to understand, it took me years to gather all these things together. We all know so very little of the simple, simple things that I am bringing before you. Yet, if we would just take heed to what God says, I declare, there would be a revival among the saints.

The Baptism in the Spirit

A Mystery

One of the interesting things, which we have already noticed, when reading Revelation, chapter 1, is that the Churches are called, 'a Mystery'. Why should they be called this? What I want to do, for a little while, is to show you why, these little companies of persons, who are saved by grace, are looked upon as a Mystery. Then, maybe, we will understand what the Assembly, the Local Church, is all about.

The very first simple thing that I see, about this Mystery, is that every one of these seven lampstands is complete in itself. Sometimes we read about chandeliers, these things that hang down from the ceiling, with all their rows of lamps. Now, this lampstand was not that sort of a thing. In some homes today we see candelabra on the table, with the various branches, but a lampstand is not like that, either. It was one single lampstand. It stood absolutely alone. Now, the like of this was never known in Old Testament times. This is absolutely different. God never intended the Church at Ephesus to interfere in any way with the Church at Pergamos; and He never intended the Church at Pergamos to interfere with the Church at Ephesus. Each one stands altogether, and absolutely, on its own base.

Church Principles for Today

Each one is responsible to God, and to God alone, for its government, testimony, conduct and discipline. I wish we could understand it! Indeed, woe betide the Assembly that interferes in the affairs of another. And woe betide the evangelist who interferes with an Assembly's affairs. And woe betide the patriarch who interferes in an Assembly's affairs. And woe betide the missionary, or trustee, or teacher, that interferes in an Assembly's affairs. They are doing despite to the simple truth of God.

Many times, in my wanderings among the Assemblies, overseeing brethren come to me and say, "Look, Mr. Jennings, we have a problem. Can you help us?" Now that is something I dread anybody asking me. Time and again I have said with all the grace that was given to me, that I never interfere in an Assembly's affairs. If you want me to minister the Scriptures, I will do my best to do so, but do not ask me to go into the affairs of the Assembly. That is the responsibility of that Church, and that Church alone.

Sometimes when I go into Assemblies, I see things that are done in one which could not be done in another. I never interfere. It is none of my business. If the Assembly gives me the

The Baptism in the Spirit

authority to teach the truth of Holy Scripture, as I plainly see it, I will do so, but I have no right to interfere in any of its affairs.

There is no central government of Assemblies. None. Assemblies which are gathered together, through a central government, might find out what to do about individual matters, but are going absolutely against the revealed will of God. He demands every one to stand on its own base. It is what we sometimes call, "autonomous".

Now, is that not a wonderful thing? God expects you to close your eyes to every other Assembly in the whole wide world and expects everybody else to close their eyes to you. If a problem comes into one meeting ... (I can begin to see God's mind in this, can you?)... other Churches do not interfere, they are not allowed to, and so the problem is localised. It will not spread. Can you see that? Whereas, if there is a central government and a problem arises somewhere, it is brought to that central government and it affects everyone, and before you know it, that problem is spread across the whole world and every member in that particular organisation is involved. God says, 'I want strength, and strength is not in unity.'

Church Principles for Today

God never wanted a world Church system; He never wanted the amalgamation of Churches; He never wanted the amalgamation of Assemblies and He does not want the ecumenical movement. God demands that every Church must stand completely, and absolutely, on its own. I tell you, if we learned that truth, and put it into practice, there would be less trouble!

Another thing you would notice, perhaps, is that there were seven lampstands, all similar to each other. This shows perfectly clearly not only that each Assembly should stand on its own but yet there is an interdependence. God never expected the one Local Church to evangelise the whole world! So there is an interdependence, and the meeting up the street, and the one down the street, are together working for the spread of the Gospel. So, in one sense, they do need one another, they are dependant upon one another, but not in government.

If we were to look at these little Assemblies, for a while, we would see that they were almost in the form of a circle and right in the very midst of the circle is the Lord, but outside, a dark world (See Figure 3.1). Every individual Assembly is looking in to Christ in the middle, and looking out to the world that is dark.

The Baptism in the Spirit

If you were to look again at these seven Churches, for a moment or two, you would see that they are all made of gold. Every Assembly had their origin in God, for gold is the metal of deity.

Figure 3.1: **The Seven Churches of Asia**

One day someone asked me to differentiate between what is an Assembly and what is not, and to explain just when an Assembly is no longer an Assembly. Would you do that? You can if you wish, but do not ask me! Would it not be an awful thing, if I said something disrespectful about a meeting of believers that had its origin in God? Now, I am not teaching liberalism. Indeed, I am teaching the very opposite!

Church Principles for Today

We are dealing with the Church of God as regards to its origin. We are dealing with the Church of Christ as to its relationship .We cannot say to God, "Do not do this", or "Do not do that".

If you went around as many Assemblies as I do, you would find they differ as face to face. A number of the places that we might not be happy with are in some respects, perhaps, nearer to Scripture than others. So it is not our job to interfere with another company of believers, either individually, or collectively. Let them look after themselves – before God. This is what it means to be autonomous. Each lampstand, representing that Church, was all of gold, they had their origin with God.

You will notice that they did not take upon themselves the name of any man. They did not say, 'I am of Paul, this is the Church of Paul', or 'This is the Church of Peter', or 'This is the Baptist Church' (with due respect), or 'This is the Lutheran Church', or 'This is the Presbyterian Church', or even 'These are the Brethren'. Every one of them just assumed the title God gave it, 'a Church'. As soon as you attach a name to your Church, you take away from the One who originated it and instead of looking at Him you are looking only at the channel.

The Baptism in the Spirit

Woe betide us if we begin to call our little Assemblies by the names of men, or doctrines, or forms of gathering together. As soon as we begin to do that, we immediately become a circle and the autonomy is broken.

> Which Assembly do you belong too?
> "Oh, I belong to the Presbyterians."
> "Well, which do you belong too?"
> "I belong to the Brethren."
> "And you?"
> "Oh, I go to the Covenanters."

Do you see all the little names? And what is very serious is that we might then say that if you do not go to my group, to my sort of Church, to my ring of Assemblies, then I can have no fellowship with you.

Once we begin to give ourselves names, we immediately do away with the autonomy of the individual Assembly.

Not only that, but we find that each one of these little lampstand-Assemblies depended entirely upon oil for its shining. (They were not candlesticks, but they were lamp stands.)

Church Principles for Today

We know that oil is an emblem of the Holy Spirit of God and as such we are solely dependent upon Him. As soon as you look to men you are lost. Do we not sometimes imagine that if we had a particular brother in our Assembly, what an asset that would be? Whenever we look to a man, no matter who it is, should it be the greatest soul upon the face of the Earth, we are not depending on the Holy Spirit of God. If there is going to be any blessing in your meeting make sure you get the oil of the Holy Spirit. But what a lovely thing it would be to have all these gifted brethren amongst us? Do not depend on them! They are only channels, that is all. The greatest of them – only channels.

Paul, in writing to the believers in Corinth, devoted four whole chapters with this very thing. In chapter 3, he asks, 'Who am I?' Why, this is the mighty Paul! Then he asks, in chapter 1, 'Was I crucified for you? I am only a man. Oh, it is true that I plant, it is true that Apollos waters, but without God there would be no growth.' Could we get our eyes off the brethren, our eyes off men, our eyes off teachers, our eyes off human beings, great and mighty though they may be, and ensure we get our support from the Holy Spirit of God, and Him alone? Maybe we would then begin to shine. That is exactly what it says, in I Corinthians, chapter 3.

The Baptism in the Spirit

Then, if you would read a bit more carefully, you would find that each one of these little candlesticks had a star. Now I am not going to explain that, but it is perfectly clear that this star is symbolic of the brethren who take control of the meeting: Those brethren (in the plural) who are sometimes referred to as elders, sometimes as overseers, sometimes as bishops and sometimes as shepherds. God has not ordained one, but many, to this office.

It is no wonder that it was called, a "Mystery". There was not the like of such a thing in the whole of Old Testament times – not even in the days of the Maccabees when the synagogues sprouted up all over Jewry. If only we would take heed.

Chapter 4

The Gifts of the Spirit

Our reading for this chapter will be in:

The First Epistle of Paul, to the Corinthians, chapter 14, verses 20-21:

"Brethren, be not children in understanding: howbeit in malice be ye children, but in understanding be men. In the law it is written, With men of other tongues and other lips will I speak unto this people; and yet for all that will they not hear me, saith the Lord."

Church Principles for Today

Introduction

As we come to the subject of Spiritual Gifts, as we sometimes call them, we need to ask ourselves a very simple question: When we hear the Ministers of the Word, speaking about Spiritual Gifts, what do they mean?

I remember one time, in England, many years ago, I was over taking some ministry meetings, and the brethren came to me and said, "We would appreciate it if, tonight, after the Gospel Meeting, when the Assembly is together, that you tell us about Spiritual Gifts." Now, I had never ministered on the subject before and I had some very quick thinking to do.

When I came into the meeting, to give the lecture, I noticed, to my horror, two esteemed and very well known teachers, whom I knew personally, were there. So I went over to them and said, "I am going to speak on Spiritual Gifts, this evening, and I want you, please, to listen to every word that I say, and when the meeting is over I want you to be really critical of my handling of the subject. Hurtfully critical! I want you to tell me, plainly, whether I was right or wrong."

The Gifts of the Spirit

(The fact, of whether they would agree or disagree, with what I said, would not, of course, indicate that I was right or wrong!)

After the meeting, I had the conversation with both of them, and I asked them for their opinion, to which they replied, "Correct!"

This, of course, gave me great encouragement. Since then, other beloved brethren, who I also esteem, say I am altogether wrong. I feel that I am altogether right, and until I am proved wrong, by Scripture, I will teach it.

The night I was saved, on the 21st May, 1935, did God give me a Gift of the Spirit that I never had before? I know that He gave me eternal life, which I never had before. I know He gave me a new nature, that I never had before. I know He gave me a love for God, and for His people, and that I never had before (although it has to be developed); I know He gave me a love for the Scriptures and that I certainly never had before; but did He give me what we call, a "Spiritual Gift"? The answer to that question is either, "Yes", or "No"!

If you were to examine your heart, and ask yourself, "What have I now that I did not have before I was saved, in the area of Spiritual Gifts?" You could become distressed! Some of our brethren have been known never to open their mouths in any public gathering. Never even once! They have never given out a hymn. Never prayed. They have never taken any active part. They just come to the meeting and go home again. Where is the Gift? Therefore, we come to this vital question: If a person has no Gift - is he not saved? If every single soul gets a Spiritual Gift, the moment he is saved, but that Gift is not in evidence, then is he saved at all? So, we begin to measure our salvation according to our Gifts. These are the kinds of things that I dread.

Miraculous Spiritual Gifts

When we go to the New Testament Scriptures we find that the Spirit of God gave miraculous Spiritual Gifts. However, I have yet to find, in the New Testament, where it says that He gave them the moment the person was saved!

If we were to turn to the three places in the New Testament

The Gifts of the Spirit

Scriptures where it speaks of these things: The Epistle to the Romans, chapter 12, the Epistle to I Corinthians, chapter 12 and the Ephesians, chapter 4, we would find that it does not intimate, in any one of them, that those Spiritual Gifts mentioned, were received at the moment of salvation.

I would ask you a very simple question: Are you using up your life trying to find what your Gift is? Surely, if God gave you a Spiritual Gift, the moment that you were saved, then it should be seen in you before now!

You, therefore, must begin to ask yourself whether those special Gifts were for the time, then present, and whether God continues to give them still? This is a very solemn question and it must only be answered by recourse to the Scriptures themselves.

Let us look, then, at one or two of these Spiritual Gifts, which were miraculously given to the young saints of that day, and see just exactly what they were for.

There was one Gift, in the New Testament Scriptures, called

Church Principles for Today

Revelation (although it is never actually called, "a Spiritual Gift," yet, it was something God did give to man). It is clear to see that when you study this Gift of Revelation, that it is not something you can conjure up; it is not something you can learn; it is not something that is inherent in you. Some think that there are people today who have this Gift, so let us look at it for a while.

We find in the Book of Leviticus, chapter 24, that Moses became involved in a dispute about an Israeli woman and an Egyptian man. The people came to him and asked him.

'What are we going to do? Here is an Egyptian man and an Israeli woman and they have married. According to the law, these things ought never to be. The Egyptian is a Gentile. What shall we do Moses?'

Moses said, 'I do not know. I really have no idea what we should do!'

He had never come across an incident like that before. 'But,' he said, 'I will tell you what we will do. We will put them into safe custody and we will ask the mind of the Lord.' And that is what he did. The Egyptian man and the Israeli woman, who had been found together, were put in ward until the mind of the

The Gifts of the Spirit

Lord could be known. So, by a process, that is not told us, God made known to the man, Moses, what he ought to do. He revealed His mind on the subject. So, Moses obeyed and he stoned them.

Now, say, that in the next week another Israeli woman who had been found with another Egyptian man, what would Moses have done? Would he had said to put them in ward until he would know the mind of the Lord? Not at all! He had written it down as soon as the incident happened and what was then revealed, and from now on that which was written down in the Word of God, only had to be read and obeyed. Never again, would God reveal to Moses what to do in a similar incident.

It is not very long afterwards, in Numbers, chapter 15, where a man was out, on the Sabbath Day, gathering sticks.
'What are we going to do with him?
'I do not know,' said Moses, 'The only thing we can do is to put him in ward, until we know the mind of the Lord.'
So they did that and waited for a Revelation from the Lord.

Whatever means this process of Revelation took, we do not

know, but somehow God made known to Moses, what he should do. He might have revealed it by literally speaking to him. God could have said to Moses, 'You have found a man chopping sticks on the Sabbath Day? Stone the man!' That is the way God could have done it, because it tells us plainly, that God did not speak to Moses in riddles, but spoke to him face to face. In any case, God was revealing His heart to the man, He was revealing His mind, He was revealing His judgement. He may have done it through the Holy Spirit or by a dream. But whatever means was used, Moses understood the will of the Lord, and had the man stoned. Then he wrote it down. You will never have to put a man in ward again for a similar crime.

Can you see what has happened? God has revealed his mind to His people by a Word of Revelation, the people wrote it down, and then all they have to do, afterwards, is to read it and obey.

We do not know the way God revealed Himself, but we do know that if we want to understand the mind of God, then there is only one way it can be known and that is by God's self-revelation. If God did not reveal Himself, we could never find Him out. Never! There is not one professor, in any university,

The Gifts of the Spirit

that could find out one jot, or tittle, about God. Such knowledge cannot be found by science, or by experiments, or from history. You cannot find God by thinking, and certainly not be intelligence. The only way to find God is by His own self-revelation.

Let us see what happens in the Epistle to the Ephesians, chapter 3. Listen to what Paul says, 'Ye know that by Revelation, God has made known unto me the Mystery of the Church, which I wrote, which when ye read, ye should understand my knowledge, in the Mystery of Christ.' There it is! God has made known, to Paul, by Revelation, he wrote it down, you read it and understand it.

So, God's Revelation is absolutely complete and no one today, anywhere, ever gets a Revelation from God. This Gift of the Spirit, let me tell you, was done away with years ago. It has ended because the Bible - God's inspired Revelation of Himself - is complete.

When you hear the beloved teaching brethren talking about having a thing revealed to them, really, honestly, they should be using the word, "illumination". It was there all the time. It has already been revealed, but now the Word has been opened up to them and they see it. It has been illuminated to them.

If you would stand up and say, "But God did reveal this to me" then if He did, He has revealed His heart and mind to you, and the sooner we get it into the Scriptures, the better. For, if He has revealed His will, then we all should know about it. Let us get it into the Bible, right away!

You would not dare to put anything which you say God has revealed to you into the Scriptures! Would you? It says, in the Book of the Revelation, 'Cursed is the man that adds anything to this Book'.

No, the days of Revelation are over, as far as this Earth is concerned, and whatever kind of Gift of the Spirit you might think you have, there is one Gift that you have not received and it is Revelation. That is finished.

We could take another Gift, the Word of Prophesy. As far as this Gift was concerned, although slightly different to the Gift of Revelation, it was, again, God making known His mind, for

The Gifts of the Spirit

a particular situation. Something arose in an Assembly, and they did not know what to do. God made known His mind through the spiritual Gift of Prophesy.

Do we need that Gift today? No! Why? Because we have all of God's mind, and will, in the Holy Scriptures. What we have, therefore, got to do, is to read them, then to understand them. We do not need prophets today.

What about Tongues? Was there not a Gift of Tongues, in those days? Oh yes! It was a Spiritual Gift. Is that for today?

In chapter 3, we found that the Gift of Tongues is spoken of, in chapter 2, of the Acts of the Apostles, in chapter 10 and, finally, in chapter 19 and alluded to in chapter 8. Why was the Gift of Tongues given in those early days? Will God give this Gift to any man, or woman, today? In order to answer that, we had to ask ourselves why Tongues were originally given.

Why were Tongues given, in Acts, chapter 2? Certainly, not to preach the Gospel! Tongues were never given to preach the Gospel. The reason why Tongues were given was to prove that

Church Principles for Today

the Holy Spirit of God had come down to Earth, to take up His abode.

Now, let me ask you a question: The very moment you were saved and the Spirit of God entered your body - did you feel Him enter? Do not be ashamed to answer that. Did you feel the Holy Spirit enter your body? The answer is that you most certainly did not! That instant, in which you were saved, did you experience a trembling come over you because the very Spirit of God had entered your body? That did not happen to you, either!

I am surprised, that when we come to the Acts of the Apostles, chapter 19, we read,

'Have you received the Holy Spirit?'

'Holy Spirit? We did not even know that He had come!'

I tell you, the Jews knew He had come. You see, you cannot see the Holy Spirit. You cannot see Him entering into a person, nor see Him taking possession of a person. The way that God used, in those early days, to show that the Spirit of God had come down from Heaven, to take up His dwelling place amongst men, was that He wrought the miracle of Tongues.

The Gifts of the Spirit

Tell me, do you need that? Do you need to talk in Tongues, before you know that the Spirit of God has taken up His dwelling place in your body? No! Why? Because, Romans chapter 8, says, 'If the Spirit of God is not in you, you are not saved at all'. I am telling you, that we do not need Tongues today, in order to show us that the Spirit of God has taken up His place in us. We have the Scripture to prove it - and that is far better than Tongues, to me!

If I should suddenly get the Gift of Tongues, I would be afraid, I would begin to tremble on my feet. I am glad that I have never demonstrated the coming of the Spirit into my life, by Tongues, because I would have been afraid of the source. But I am not afraid of the source of the Scriptures. If God says that He will give the Spirit to me, when I trust Him, then that is good enough for me!

If someone asks, "But why did God ever use such a strange thing as an unknown Tongue?" The answer is made perfectly clear, in I Corinthians, chapter 14, verse 2, 'That even by these strange Tongues, God made known His mind'. It was a form of Revelation, just as Prophesy was a form of Revelation. So Tongues was a way that God used to reveal His heart. But I know God's mind - I have the Scriptures - therefore, I do not need Tongues! If we were to go to the Tongues Movement, as we have in I Corinthians, chapter 14, it would be easy to explain that, from the context of the passage.

Therefore, there is no need for Tongues, today; there is no need for Revelation, today; there is no need for Prophesy, today.

Then, there was another Gift: It was the Gift, called "Knowledge". Now, that particular Gift was to know, without having ever learned.

I would love that Gift. Imagine, going to bed at night knowing absolutely nothing about the Epistle to the Romans, and wakening in the morning, knowing the lot! What a delightful way to learn. Imagine, being able to know every jot, and tittle, of the whole of the Book of the Revelation, having never even read it. That is the Gift of Knowledge.

Now, I want to tell you sensible people that, that Gift is gone, also. In the days of the New Testament, because the New Tes-

The Gifts of the Spirit

tament was not yet complete, God had to give a man the Gift of Knowledge, having never learned. It was a miraculous Gift. It was a Gift, direct from the Spirit of God. The man knew the thing, having never learned it.

Is that the way we learn today? I want to tell you that the only way to get Knowledge, today, whether it be of God, or anything else, is to spend hours, and hours, of reading, of writing, of studying, of meditating, of thinking, of listening; to spend hours of burning the midnight oil, day in, day out, year in, year out, without end. That is the only way to get to know anything - spiritual, or otherwise! There is no other way. Some are quick at learning, others are slow, but there is no easy way. Only by study.

Then, God caused the men to write down what they knew. So, what men understood from Prophesy, from Revelation, from Tongues, from Knowledge, as given by God, having never learned, they wrote down and we have it in the form of our Bible. Now the question is, how are we going to learn?

I am going to tell you how you get to know the mind of God. Never think that today you will know the mind of God, by

Church Principles for Today

Revelation. You will not! Never think that you will learn the mind of God, by Tongues, neither will you learn by the Gift of Knowledge. What we do today is read and teach, and by reading and teaching, we learn God's mind. All I am doing, at this instant, is giving to you the understanding of what is plainly written in His Word. I am not giving you a Revelation; I am not Prophesying; I am not speaking in Tongues; I have no Gift of Knowledge, but I have read and I am seeking to teach. It is then the job of the reader to try to understand and to put it into practice. That is God's order for today. Consequently, as the Canon of Scripture is complete, we do not need these, nor any other miraculous Gifts, to express God's wishes for us.

Spiritual Gifts for Today

Then I ask myself, what is the operation of God, today? It is the same today, as in those bygone days, even of the days of the above Gifts.

(This is where I begin to differ with some of my beloved brethren, but I put it to you for your consideration.)

I am going to suggest to you that you have, what I am going

The Gifts of the Spirit

to call, "a Natural Gift". Some people are born with good brains, some are not; some people are born with the Gift of Helping, others are not; some people are good at visiting the sick, others would, perhaps, be better not; some are good at welcoming people at the door of the hall, others not; some are good at this, some are good at that, and there will always be some wee thing that you have, which someone else has not got. We call them, "Natural Gifts".

Who gave them to you? Do you not think that it was God who gave them to you? Surely, every good, and perfect, Gift, is from Him?

What should I do with my Natural Gift? Sanctify it!

Sanctify it? Let us see just what that word means. (It certainly does not only mean to make holy. There is more to it than that!) What does it mean to sanctify your Natural Gifts? It means to set them apart, for God.

Can we find substantiation for that in the New Testament? Of course, we can, for it is full of beautiful examples. Yonder,

Church Principles for Today

in the Epistle to the Romans, chapter 5, what did these hands do before I was saved? I used them for the works of unrighteousness. What do I use them for, today? I take them, those very same hands, and dedicate them to the use of my Lord.

Oh, what a clever brain, you have. How quick you can learn. You just look at a thing once and you understand it. In school, you were always first in class, top of the list every time. I say, before you were saved you used your brain for your own advancement, but look what happened? You use that same brain for God; use that same quick-thinking Gift, to look at, and study, the Word.

There is no end to what one could say about Gifts. There is plenty of room for all those Natural Gifts, that are sanctified.

A very eloquent brother said to me, one time, "Rowan, I can remember many years ago walking along a road, I could show you the very spot, when the thought came into my heart - I am going to dedicate my life to teach the Word of God". He sanctified his Gift. Instead of running about wondering about what kind of a Spiritual Gift God ever gave us, we have Gifts galore, and at our very fingertips, and all God wants us to do is get

The Gifts of the Spirit

those Natural Gifts and sanctify them to His use.

Is there anything like that in the New Testament? Romans, chapter 6, is full of it. Read it yourself and see, 'Set aside those Gifts you have, those members of yours, which used to be members of unrighteousness, and sanctify them, now, for the Master's use".

I delight, at times, to find the character of the men who wrote the New Testament. I would find that wonderful man, Matthew, was an income-tax man, and he used to build up his coins into little piles. Can you imagine going to the cashier, in a bank, where all the coins, and notes, were scattered all over the place? It would take the cashier an hour to give you the change. No, he takes a few coins from one pile and a few from another pile, and before you know where you are, he has the change in his hand. Why? Because he has them all set out into little piles. Matthew was a tax gatherer. He loved to put things into little piles and when he begins to write the Gospel of Matthew he just cannot get away from it. Mark is not like that. He scatters things all over the place (although for a purpose, and as guided by the Holy Spirit). But not Matthew. He takes five miracles and puts them all together, in chapter 8. Then, in chapter 9, he

Church Principles for Today

has more miracles. Can you guess how many he has there? If he has five miracles, in chapter 8, then he has got to have five, in chapter 9. His little piles must be right, you understand.

When he starts, in chapter 1, he talks about generations, but he counts them to make fourteen.

'What a delightful little pile, Matthew. Are you going to make another pile?'

'Yes. I will make another.'

'How many in this next pile then? Eighteen'?'

'Oh, no. Take four away from the top, so as to make this second pile, of names, the same as the first!'

Another little pile, of fourteen. 'What are you doing, Matthew?'

'I am building little piles.'

You see, the tax collector is coming out, his Gift of building things into piles has been sanctified.

What is he doing, in chapters 5,6 and 7? He is building more piles. What is he doing in chapter 17? More little piles! What is he doing, in chapters 24 and 25? More little piles. The man cannot get away from building those little piles. The Natural Gift,

The Gifts of the Spirit

sanctified for God.

Now, you will not find any piles, like that, in the Gospel according to Luke. And who is he? A physician! A doctor. I am glad that there was one Gospel writer who was a doctor. Mary told those delicate things, about her experiences leading up to the birth of the Lord, to Doctor Luke. She would never have told those things to Matthew, the tax collector, nor to John, the fisherman.

One day, Doctor Luke came to a man who had leprosy. He recognised, immediately, what his problem was and knew just what to say. He states what none of the rest of the Gospel writers knew to say, 'He was *full* of leprosy'. You only have to read that delightful Gospel, to see the doctor coming out in it everywhere. What has God done? He has taken the medical expertise of this man, Luke, and sanctified it for His own use.

You can take that dear fisherman, John. You will find that he loved to work with his father: He and his father used to go out and fish together; he and his father used to go and mend the nets together. He was a lad who loved to work with his father. God did not miss that and, one day, He said to John,

Church Principles for Today

'John, I want you to write Me a book.'

'What will this book be about, Lord?'

'It will be about the Person of the Lord Jesus, John. Write about My Son and I. Write about My Son and His Father working together, John.'

So, John took up his pen and began to write. What is he writing about? He is writing about a Son who knows how to work with His Father. What is the Lord doing? He is taking that Natural Gift of the man and sanctifying it!

I wish I could sanctify my Gift! That is exactly where the Spirit of God comes in. Not that He is going to give you something you never had before but, rather, the Spirit of God will take what you have and sanctify it, and use it, for God.

Who was Paul, the Apostle, before he was saved? He was a lawyer. He used to sit, in his unsaved days, at the feet of Gamaliel, the teacher. In his day, he would have been, I suppose, a Doctor of Philosophy. A highly educated academic, one who knew how to ask the most searching of questions. Then, one

The Gifts of the Spirit

day, God saved him and took up his pen to write the Epistle to the Romans. Read it and count the questions. Not ten, not twenty, not thirty, more than forty, more than fifty, more than sixty, more than seventy questions. There are seventy-six questions throughout this book. He is asking questions, searching questions, all the way through. It is the book of the lawyer. It is a book of legal things. John, the fisherman, could not have written it. Matthew, the tax collector, could not have written it. Paul, the lawyer, could. Can you see what God is doing? Even in the days of those miraculous Spiritual Gifts? God is taking the Natural Gifts, which He has given to men, and the training which those men had and has sanctified them to His use.

Could I ask you, then, to forget about Spiritual Gifts, as such, and to look to see what kind of a Natural Gift you have? The Gift of visitation? The Gift of a cheery word? The Gift of helping? The Gift of hospitality? Whatever your Gift is, would you like to say, from this moment on, "This is for you, Lord. The next time I entertain someone, I am going to do it as if this person were the Lord, Himself!" Sanctify that which you know you have, for Him.

Church Principles for Today

Rewards

Will the Lord reward you? Of course, He will! How do I know? Because it has been revealed in His Word, and we have only to read the Epistle to the Colossians, and there it says, 'Whatsoever you do, do it unto Him and He is no respecter of persons, and of Him you will receive that, "Well done", by and by!

Can I work in the home like that? Yes! Can I work in the office like that? Yes! It is not the first time, when in the simplicity of my poor little mind, I am about to throw a paper clip into the waste bin, when I stop and ask myself, whether the Lord would throw other people's property away! I could not see Him doing such a thing and, so, I put it in the drawer for further use. What a tiny thing! Do you mean to tell me that on that great Day of Review, the Lord Jesus will forget that I did that because of Him? No, not for a moment. If you would just take that little life of yours, and look for the things that you can do and sanctify them for the Master's use, you will get your reward.

In the Gospel according to Luke, chapter 7, a poor woman comes into a house. No one has any time for her, and even the

The Gifts of the Spirit

Lord seems to take no notice of her. He seems to be so busy talking to those around, and they seem to be so busy talking to Him, that you would almost think that He was taking no notice of the woman, who was at His feet: As she took ointment and poured it on His feet and, as her tears fell onto His feet, she wiped them with the hairs of her head. However, at the end of the chapter, the Lord said to Simon,

'Simon ... '

'Yes, Lord?'

'When I came into your house, you did not remove My shoes.'

'I know.'

'She did! When I came into your house, you did not anoint My feet with refreshing water. She did! When I came into your house, you did not wash My feet. She did! When I came into your house, you did not dry My feet. She did!'

Do you know what the Lord did at the end of chapter 7, of Luke's Gospel? He went over every single thing that, that woman had done, leaving nothing out. A Gift sanctified for the Master's use and will be recognised by the Lord and will be rewarded accordingly.

Church Principles for Today

Control of the Gifts

Now, I come to a question: If the Gift of Tongues is gone; if the Gift of Prophesy is gone; if the Gift of Healing is gone; then why does God leave on record such a mass of Scripture, that has got to do with these very Gifts? You might as well tear those out of your Bible! After all, what is the sense of the whole of chapter 14, of I Corinthians, which deals with the Gift of Tongues, when there are no Tongues, today?

I want to tell you, that if I were to take that Gift of Tongues, of those days, and find out how they used that Gift, then I would see how God wants me to use my Gift, today. So, that Gift which came from God, which was a Spiritual Gift, God said that it had to be used in a certain way. So, I watch which way they had to use their Gifts, and that is how I get the guidance to use my Natural Gift.

Now, when we read I Corinthians, chapter 14, in that light, and forget about Tongues, and Knowledge, and all those things, and ask ourselves these questions: 'How did they operate their Gifts?' And, 'What were the methods whereby they operated them?' Then, I Corinthians, chapter 14, will open up

The Gifts of the Spirit

in an entirely new light and I will begin to find, exactly, how I should use my Gifts.

One of the very first things that I would learn is that a Spiritual Gift must be controlled, and limited, by Scriptural usage. I think you will understand what I mean when I tell you to look at one Natural Gift as a example: What do I know about football? Very, very little! But there is one thing I do know, and that is, that there used to be a famous footballer, called George Best, who was supposed to be one of the greatest footballers of all time. Good! What a Natural Gift! Could he sanctify that for the Master's use? No! Why? Because it is beyond the control of the Holy Scripture!

So, I have to be very, very careful. Oh, I have a Natural Gift, and it came from God. I want to sanctify it. Then ask yourself the question whether it can be controlled, and sanctified, by the Spirit of God? Is it possible to sanctify all Natural Gifts to God? The answer is, 'No'!

Further, I must, as Scriptures would show, stir up the Gift that is within me. Oh, what a Gift I have for visiting the people of God. Oh, what a Gift I have ... well, are you using it? You see, if you are not using it, then you are not stirring it up. Would it not be a delightful thing, to search for your Natural Gift and then stir it up? Go ahead! Do it!

When I read these passages concerning Spiritual Gifts, there is one thing I learn about them and it is very serious. They are never to be used for self-advancement! If you are going to use that Natural Gift, of yours, to make your name great, then you are not being controlled by the Spirit of God. That is the flesh! You must not exercise these Gifts for self-aggrandisement.

But, if we were to go through chapter 14, it would be perfectly clear that the exercise of that Gift of yours, that Natural Gift, which has been sanctified, must be for the edification of the people of God, and not for the dividing of them! Would it be possible to divide the saints with true Spiritual Gifts? Yes!

Then, I would find, perfectly clearly, that before anybody teaches, he has got to learn that he cannot teach what he does not know! If you ever want to teach, then the first thing you have got to do, is to learn, and there is only one way to do that, and that is by study. There is no use trying to teach otherwise.

The Gifts of the Spirit

You will find, therefore, that your Natural Gifts can be sanctified and, not only so, but also controlled by the Holy Scripture. So, if I do as I am instructed, in I Corinthians, chapter 14, then I will be able to use my Gifts, with conviction, and know that they are acceptable to God.

Let me close, this section, with the remarks of one great man of God. Here is what he said,

"The characteristic work of the Holy Spirit in the believer today is not the impartation of miraculous Gifts but the development of Christian character."

I trust, indeed, that this is clear. Therefore, if you think that you have got a miraculous Spiritual Gift, all right, but do not teach that everybody must have one but, rather, as Romans, chapter 6, states, 'Those Gifts that have already shown themselves, sanctify them for the Master's use and, according to II Timothy, chapter 3, 'Oh, if there is a vessel then, provided that it is clean, it is fit for the Master's use!'

One day, in a Baptist Church, a young man was praying, and in his prayer, he said, "Oh, Lord, use me". After the prayer meeting, the old pastor put his arm around the young man's shoulder, and praised him, and encouraged him, then he said, "Son, if you are clean, then you will not have to ask God to use you". You keep yourself clean, you make yourself clean, and God will do the using. What a delightful thing. If I were only clean. How can I become clean? Sanctification!

Sanctification of My Gift

What is Sanctification?

This idea, of Sanctification, can be misunderstood. I remember, when I was a young man, of just 17 years and not long saved. I was full of zeal for God, but not knowing the Brethren Assemblies, not knowing the Pentecostal Church, not knowing anything, except the Presbyterian Church, I heard of two girls preaching in a tent, about Sanctification, and I went to hear them. One of them preached about how God wants our, "Full Sanctification". I thought, "This is just the very thing I have been looking for. This is the very thing that I want". So, after the meeting I went to speak to them, in order to become fully sanctified. Accordingly, I got down on my knees and prayed to be made fully holy! Poor chap! Poor girl!

The Gifts of the Spirit

I have learned an awful lot since then. I learned that if this word, "Sanctification", means, "holy", I want to tell you that I am not fully sanctified yet.

What we want to learn is, what does the Holy Spirit mean by this word, "Sanctification"? Firstly, the word, "sanctified", has not only got to do with holiness! Sometimes, it does; sometimes, it does not. In the Acts of the Apostles, one time, God said to the brethren, 'Sanctify to Me, Paul and Barnabas, for the work which I have called them'. So the word, "Sanctification", need not necessarily mean holiness. If you would read, in the Old Testament Scriptures, you would find that certain pots were sanctified! Can you make a pot holy? Indeed, even the bells on the horses neck are, one day, going to be sanctified. Can you make a bell, on a horses neck, holy? Never! Therefore, we come to the conclusion that this word, "Sanctification", means to, "set aside, or to dedicate, for use".

Oh, this brain of mine, I am going to sanctify it. I am going to set it aside for God. Or more, I am going to present my whole body, as a living sacrifice, acceptable to God. Sanctification - to set aside for God.

Church Principles for Today

Call it what you like: You can put your own words to it. You can call it, "The First Blessing"; call it, "The Second Blessing"; call it, "The Third Blessing"; you can call it, "Sanctification"; or you can call it, "Full Sanctification". I do not really mind what you call it! But there is such a thing, in the Christian life, as a dedication of that life. Ask any of those brethren who have gone across the seas, as missionaries, and they will tell you that at such a time, in their lives, they set themselves aside for God. Sanctification: A setting aside.

In the Gospel of John, the Person of the Lord Jesus Christ, said, 'I sanctify Myself'. The Lord sanctifying Himself? Do you, honestly, mean that the Lord was to make Himself holy? Of course, that is not the meaning! You do not mean to tell me that the Lord Jesus was going to sin less! Such a thing would be blasphemous! When He said that, then, what did He mean?

The Lord said that there was a work to be done, in Heaven. He said, 'I am going away. I am going away and you will be left down here. Oh, there will be troubles, sorrows and tribulations, which you will experience, down here, but I am going to leave you, nevertheless. I am going to go away up there. But, I want to tell you what I am going to do, for you, when I get up there. I

The Gifts of the Spirit

am going to set myself apart for you. I am going to live for you; I am going to pray for you; I am going to work for you; not for the angels, nor for the cherubim, not even for the seraphim, but for you.' That is how He sanctified Himself. It was a setting of Himself apart.

Of course, there are cases when it does mean holiness. Sanctification can have three meanings, if you like: It can have this ethical meaning, that is, simply setting something, or someone, apart for a task; it can mean a separation from something; and it can mean a separation to something.

May the Lord help us to live sanctified lives, to Him.

Chapter 5

Baptism

Before we study the beautiful subject of Baptism, I would like to quote from:

I Corinthians, chapter 10, verses 1 - 4:

"Moreover, brethren, I would not that that ye should be ignorant, how that all our fathers were under the cloud, and all passed through the sea; And were all baptised unto Moses in the cloud and in the sea; And did all eat the same spiritual meat; And did all drink the same spiritual drink: for they drank of that spiritual Rock that followed them: and that Rock was Christ."

Then, in verse 11:

"Now all these things happened unto them for ensamples: and they are written for our admonition, upon whom the ends of the world are come."

Then, in the Epistle to the Romans, chapter 6, verses 1 - 9:

"What shall we say then? Shall we continue in sin, that grace may abound? God forbid. How shall we, that are dead to sin, live any longer therein? Know ye not, that so many of us as were baptised into Jesus Christ were baptised into his death? Therefore we are buried with him by baptism into death: that like as Christ was raised up from the dead by the glory of the Father, even so we also should walk in newness of life. For if we have been planted together in the likeness of his death, we shall be also in the likeness of his resurrection: Knowing this, that our old man is crucified with him, that the body of sin might be destroyed, that henceforth we should not serve sin. For he that is dead is freed from sin. Now if we be dead with Christ, we believe that we shall also live with him: Knowing that Christ being raised from the dead dieth no more; death hath no more dominion over him."

And finally, in I Peter, chapter 3, verses 15 - 22:

"But sanctify the Lord God is your hearts: and be ready always to give an answer to every man that asketh you a reason of the hope that is in you with meekness and fear: Having a good conscience; that, whereas they speak evil of you, as of evildoers, they may be ashamed that falsely accuse your good conversation in Christ. For it is better, if the will of God be so, that ye suffer for well doing, than for evil doing. For Christ also hath once suffered for sins, the just for the unjust, that he might bring us to God, being put to death in the flesh, but quickened by the Spirit: By which also he went and preached unto the spirits in prison; Which sometime were disobedient, when once the long-suffering of God waited in the days of Noah, while the ark was a preparing, wherein few, that is, eight souls were saved by water. The like figure whereunto even baptism doth also now save us (not the putting away of the filth of the flesh, but the answer of a good conscience toward God,) by the resurrection of Jesus Christ: Who is gone into heaven, and is on the right hand of God; angels and authorities and powers being made subject unto him."

Church Principles for Today

Introduction

Now, we have already seen in our studies that there is such a thing called the Church and that there are those things called Churches. Connected to these two beautiful pictures, or symbols, there are two Ordinances. There is, first of all, that which is called the Ordinance of Baptism and, then, there is what is called the Ordinance of the Breaking of Bread, or sometimes we call it, 'The Lord's Supper'. I am going to deal with these two Ordinances: The first one, Baptism, in this chapter and the next one, the Lord's Supper, in chapter 6. It may be that you have heard these lectured on so many times that, you declare, there is nothing new to be learned. But I am not just too sure that, that is altogether correct. We may, perhaps, see if we look at these things just one more time, a point, or so, that we may not have noticed before.

The first thing you might notice is that when you get the institution of something in the Gospels, then read of its practice in the Acts of the Apostles, and finally get its doctrine in the Epistles, then it is an exceedingly important subject.

We shall find, when we study the Lord's Supper, that it is in-

Baptism

stituted, not in Matthew, nor in Mark, nor in John but, most definitely, in the Gospel according to Luke. We will find it was instituted there by the Lord Jesus, Himself. We will find, in the Acts of the Apostles, chapter 20, that it was practised by the apostles and we will find the doctrine of it contained in I Corinthians, chapter 11.

If I want the institution of either of these ordinances, therefore, I go to the Gospels. If I want to make sure they were practised by the early Church, I go to the Acts. But if I want to know what they mean, what the doctrine included, why they were practised, then I do not go to the Gospels, neither do I go to the Acts, I must go to the Epistles.

If you want to know why you take the Lord's Supper, then do not go to Matthew, or Mark, or Luke. If you want to know why you take the Lord's Supper, it is not in the Acts of the Apostles. If you want to know the reason why you partake of the Lord's Supper and the teaching that is underlying it, as well as the fundamental purpose of it, then you must go to the Epistles.

The very same thing applies to Baptism. We would find in

the Gospels according to Matthew and Mark, that the Lord Jesus gave a distinct commandment. He said, 'Go and baptize'. There is the institution. The Lord Jesus has plainly said it. He said, 'Go and preach the Gospel, and when you do, people will believe, and when they believe, baptize them'. So Baptism is as much part of the Gospel as the Gospel itself! Therefore, we find in the Gospels according to Matthew and Mark, that the Lord Jesus, Himself, institutes this ordinance, of Baptism.

When we go to the Acts of the Apostles we find it has been practised in chapter 2 (verse 38); then, on a number of Jews, in chapter 8 (verse 12); also, on an Ethiopian, in chapter 8 (verse 38); then, in chapter 9; as far as the Apostle Paul was concerned (verse 18); then in chapter 10, a Gentile called Cornelius was baptised verse (48); a lady called Lydia was baptised, in chapter 16 (verse 15); also a Roman jailer was baptised, in chapter 16 (verse33) and, in chapter 19 (verse 5), we find the disciples of John were baptised for a second time. (They had been baptised once, with the Baptism of John, but it was essential that they should be baptised again. I have explained why that was so, in chapter 3.)

So we find in the Acts of the Apostles this rite of Baptism,

Baptism

this Ordinance of Baptism, was carried out. But nowhere in the Acts of the Apostles will it explain why. If I want its doctrine, I must go to the Epistles.

Baptism: The Basics

Now, we would find that Baptism is brought to us in many places in the New Testament but I have chosen only three for this study. In those three passages we will be able to discover the reason why we are baptised, that is, what the underlying teaching and doctrine is.

We will find, as we study I Corinthians, chapter 10, that the meaning given to Baptism is different from the meaning in Romans, chapter 6, but we will find, when we study Romans, chapter 6, that the meaning given to it there is altogether different from that in I Peter, chapter 3. So there is not just one simple reason underlying the Ordinance of Baptism, but at least three.

First of all, let me plainly say that Baptism never saves. Now that seems to be altogether different to what we read, in I Peter, chapter 3. There it says perfectly distinctly, "The like figure whereunto even baptism doth also now save us". Therefore, on the very surface it would appear that Baptism has got something to do with salvation. We will have to explain that and we will be able to do that, I trust, without much difficulty.

Keeping that in mind, let me also plainly declare that Baptism does not add to salvation. It cannot wash away your sins, in spite of what it appears to say, in Acts, chapter 2. That will also have to be explained and that will be very easy, also. Baptism does not wash away your sin, it does not help to save you and it is not necessary for salvation.

Persons who have been saved through simple faith will go to Heaven even if they never were baptised. That does not mean to say that they should not be baptised. That is what we are going to deal with. But I am trying to emphasise that Baptism is not an essential aspect of salvation.

I can think of a man, in the New Testament, who went to Heaven and he was not baptised. I can think of a man, in the New Testament Scriptures, who was baptised and the Apostle Peter said to him, 'I perceive, Sir, that you are in the gall of bitterness and in the bond of iniquity'. I can only understand from this that, that man was not saved at all. The thief on the cross

Baptism

had no time to get baptised. He learned salvation and received it, within minutes of his death. He could not be baptised, but that day he was found in Paradise with the Lord Jesus. Therefore, I see a man who is in Heaven and was not baptised. But I also see a man who was baptised and is not in Heaven. Therefore, I can understand, conclusively, and from other Scriptures to support it, that Baptism neither saves nor helps to save.

Therefore, on the surface, there is not much purpose in the whole exercise, is there? If it does not help me to be saved and I can go to Heaven without it, then let us just forget it! Now that is where the doctrine comes in. Why must I get Baptised? Why can I not, why dare I not, forget about it? That is what we are going to see when we study Romans, chapter 6. That is what we are going to see when we study I Corinthians, chapter 10. That is what we are going to see as we study I Peter, chapter 3.

The next thing that we should notice is that the word, 'baptize', never means to go into and to come out of. Never! For those who want to be theologians, or indeed, who are theologians, doubtless you will be familiar with this. But mark, if you are going to study some facets of New Testament doctrine, it would be absolutely essential for you to appreciate that Baptism is not a going in and a coming out. Baptism is a going in should you never come out! So, if you are being baptised and you happen to die under the water, you still will have been baptised. Baptism has got to do with going down into the water but does not imply coming out. Oh, I know the night they baptised me they did take me out, and I am absolutely delighted that they did! The Epistle to the Romans dwells on the very fact that I was not kept in the water and that I did come out.

The next thing you will find, with Baptism, is that there are always four facets applied to it. This we saw in chapter 3. So, whether it is Baptism in the Spirit, or John's Baptism, or the Lord Jesus Christ's Baptism, or the Baptism of the Children of Israel in the Red Sea, or the Baptism of Believers, it does not matter.

To remind you, briefly, the first facet is that there must be somebody who is baptised. The second facet is that somebody must do the baptizing. (Sometimes the Lord Jesus Christ is the baptizer. Oh, I could point to a place where God Himself is the baptizer.) Then you must be baptised into something - and it is not always water. We read in I Corinthians, chapter 10, of people who were baptised into a cloud. We saw that in I Corinthi-

Baptism

ans, chapter 12, people were being baptised into the Spirit. So it is not always baptised in water, but it often is and it is this, that we are going to deal with. You must be baptised into something. Those generally are easy to see, but the fourth one is not so easy.

Why were you baptised? What was the reason? Now that is not so simple. That is the doctrine. Why were the Children of Israel baptised in the cloud? Why did John the Baptist, baptize the Children of Israel? Why did the Lord Jesus baptize us into the Spirit? What was the purpose? Why are you baptised with water? What is the meaning? That is the part that is difficult to get hold of, yet it is the crucial part of all Baptisms.

What we are going to do, therefore, with water baptism, is take a look at the reasons why we are baptised.

Now, I want to take you back, before we get into the body of our work, to the Epistle to the Romans, where Paul states, "That if thou shalt confess with thy mouth the Lord Jesus, and shalt believe in thine heart that God raised him from the dead, thou shalt be saved." Now, from this it is quite clear that salvation is in a package. Salvation is not one thing, but two. When you were saved, you took the Person of the Lord Jesus Christ as your Saviour. That is true. But you will please not forget that you also took Him as your Lord. You will forget that to your peril! You take Christ as your Saviour AND you take Him as your Lord, and the Scriptures never permit you to take Him as Saviour, without taking Him as Lord! The two go together, or not at all.

Would you like to study that throughout the New Testament Scripture and find it to be perfectly true? And what God has joined together, let no man put asunder. They go together.

So, you cannot be saved and do as you like. We will see this when we get into our study and more so when we study the Lord's Supper, in the next chapter.

The very first remark of Paul the Apostle on the Damascus Road, when he saw the One he had been persecuting, 'Oh,' he said, 'Lord ...' As soon as he was saved, he said, 'Lord, what wilt Thou have me to do?' The thief on the cross, when he found out his mistake, looked for salvation from the Man on the middle cross, and his very first words were, 'Lord, won't you remember me?'

Baptism

Let me tell you, for your encouragement, that the night you were saved you knew nothing about this sort of thing. I did not even know that the Bible was divided into two parts: The Old and the New Testaments. I could not have found for you John, chapter 3 and verse 16, never mind, John, chapter 5, verse 24, or John, chapter 3 and verse 36, or I John, chapter 5 and verse 12, or Matthew, chapter 11 and verse 28, or any of those other beautiful verses. I did not know there were such verses. What happened the night I was saved? I will tell you. If the Lord had asked me to walk bare-footed to Dublin, I would have done it. Oh, the night I was saved I did not have to do anything. But if someone would have asked me, "Would you take Him as your Lord, as well as your Saviour?" I would have said, "Oh, yes! Oh yes! I will take Him. I will take Him with all that goes with Him". With a willing heart I took Him.

The result of this was that there was a change in my life, if you want to put it that way. What made the change? Without knowing it, I had accepted Him as my Lord and His laws were written on my heart. I will bring that out when we study the Lord's Supper.

Will you let me emphasise it, for the moment, that Christ

puts these two together and does not separate them. 'If you want My Son as your Saviour, then you will also take My Son as your Lord. But if you will not take Him as your Lord, I am afraid, you cannot have Him as your Saviour'. You take salvation in a package or you do not take it! It is very serious.

So you were saved. One night, with an open heart, you accepted the Lord Jesus Christ as the Lord of your life. What was the first commandment He gave you? What was the very first thing He asked you to do? Nay. What was the very first thing He told you to do? Nay. What was the very first thing He commanded you to do? He said, 'Be baptised'.

But what if you say, 'I will not'. Is that not a contradiction in terms? To take Christ, as Lord, and then to refuse the very first order He gives? Something is strange about that. Oh, the night I was baptised I did not know what it was all about. Did you? The night I was baptised I knew nothing about Romans, chapter 6 - I know little about it yet. If you had asked me ten years ago to explain I Peter, chapter 3, I would not have known where to start. I Corinthians, chapter 10, was a mystery to me, maybe it still is. But I want to tell you that on the night I was baptised, I was obeying the Lord, even though I did not know what it

Baptism

meant. Is that not a lovely thing? You would not say to the Lord, "No I will not do what You tell me, at least, until I understand it". If that is the case, I am afraid you will never be baptised, for there is too much in this Ordinance for any of us to understand fully.

Let me write right across this Ordinance of Baptism: God told me. He said to me, 'You go and get baptised, son'. So I just went and did as I was told. 'God told me'. That should be sufficient for us all.

Baptism - The Doctrines

Now, let us go to the doctrine. I am going to take I Corinthians, chapter 10, and have a look but, in order to understand it, I must go right back to the Book of Exodus. Try to follow it if you can. It will all come so clear.

I will find, in the Book of Exodus, a place called Egypt: Ruled over by an exceedingly wicked prince, called Pharaoh, who had the people in bondage. In the New Testament Scriptures it would not be hard to show that we were at one time, in the world and under the domain, and dominion, of an exceedingly wicked prince called, 'the prince of this world', and he had us all in bondage. Very alike, is it not? You would think we were talking about the same thing. You are, except in a different plain. Here is a people, in the land of Egypt, under bondage to a cruel prince, and over in the New Testament there is a people, in the world, in bondage to an exceedingly cruel prince.

Suddenly, into that land of Egypt comes a man, called Moses, and he tells the people that he is going to deliver them and bring them to a land that is flowing with milk and honey. Would that not be a beautiful thing to people in bondage? Suddenly, into this world there comes this man, called Jesus Christ, our Lord, who tells us He is going to deliver us and bring us to another land, a land that flows with milk and honey, far, far away. Is that not lovely, also?

But will you notice just one, or two, simple things? From the land of bondage to the land that flowed with milk and honey, there was a waste, howling wilderness. (Oh, what a lovely thing it would be to trace the Children of Israel going through that wilderness and find it in the Gospel of John in every single chapter, from chapter 1 through to chapter 21). We were in the

Baptism

world and we are going to a land flowing with milk and honey, but never forget that we are now in a waste, howling wilderness.

But there is another problem and it was that these people, in the land of Egypt, were not only held under the bondage of an exceedingly wicked prince but, more importantly, they were sinners before God. That was more serious. (Now, follow the argument and you will see I Corinthians, chapter 10, as plain as noonday.) Here, we were in the world, held under the bondage of an exceedingly wicked king, the prince of this world; the Lord Jesus Christ has come to deliver us and bring us safely through this waste, howling wilderness, into the land which flows with milk and honey; but we must not forget that we were also sinners.

Now, we understand that in the Book of Exodus, God must, first of all, be satisfied regarding the sin question before He will begin to guide us. When we come to the New Testament Scriptures, God must again be satisfied before the Lord Jesus begins to lead us. Let me explain that. How were the sins of the people taken care of in the land of Egypt? By the blood of the Paschal Lamb. How are our sins taken care of in the New Testament? By the blood of the Paschal Lamb: Christ our Saviour.

Now we are coming to the crux of the argument. The blood of the Paschal Lamb saved the people from their sins before God, but did not save them from the bondage of Pharaoh. Can you see that? Follow the story and you will see it!

After the blood of the Paschal Lamb was shed, and after the night of terror was over, and after the Children of Israel had taken themselves to the Red Sea, who comes after them, but Pharaoh, with all his hosts! What is he going to do? Bring them right back again! Is there anyone to save them from being brought back? The Paschal Lamb? Nay, verily, that was for God. The blood is always for God. Always and ever. The blood of the Lord Jesus Christ was never shed to satisfy you. Never! The blood of the Lord Jesus Christ was shed to be a propitiation before God. What would this man Pharaoh have done with those Children of Israel? He would have taken them right back again into the land of Egypt and they would have been in bondage all over again. Free from their sins – but still in bondage. How did they escape the bondage of Pharaoh? Now we have it! They were baptised in the sea. Can you see it?

Baptism

There they are standing beside the Red Sea. Look at them. Before them is the Red Sea, behind them Pharaoh with all his hosts. Who is going to save them? They cry unto the Lord, 'Who will save us'? I Corinthians, chapter 10, tells you what happened. They were baptised unto Moses in the sea. What does that plainly tell you, when you study the story? That the Lord said, 'If you want to be rid of the bondage of this wicked prince, follow Moses; take him as your guide, follow him; whatever he says unto you, do it'. What did Moses do? He struck the Red Sea, it parted, Moses walked through on dry land and the people walked in after him. They all passed through and came out the other side. Pharaoh went in after them, with all his hosts, but was drowned. He cannot capture them now! What has happened? They have been baptised unto Moses, as leader, as the lord of their life.

Now, let us see what I Corinthians, chapter 10, is all about. I think we can see it ourselves already! Apart from the theologians who know it inside out, what about the rest of us, can we see it in our own minds and hearts?

The Lord Jesus Christ shed His blood for me. I took Christ as my Saviour. But that did not deliver me from the bondage of the devil? Do you not know that the devil is walking about as a roaring lion seeking whom he may devour? This is not the Age when the devil is bound in the abyss. The devil is very, very wide awake. I tell you, that while the gates of Hell cannot prevail against the Church, which is His Body, as we saw in chapter 2, it can prevail against the Local Assembly and it can prevail against you, as an individual. Before another week has rolled its course, God alone knows what the devil will do with you. So, these things are very serious.

One night in the Gospel according to Luke, the Lord Jesus said to Peter,

'Oh, Peter, Peter, Peter, the devil has desired thee and before this night is over he is going to sift thee as one would sift wheat'.

Poor Peter.

'Are you going to let him, Lord?'

'Yes.'

I could tell you why[1]. It is a lovely study to find out why the Lord Jesus allowed it, but He did and before that night was over, I tell you, Peter went through the mill and shed bitter, bit-

---

1. This was discussed in detail in Mr. Jennings book, "Future Events".

ter tears. He never forgot what he had learned. Then the Lord said to Peter,

'But Peter, when you are converted'.

'Will I be converted Lord?'

'Of course, you will.'

'How do you know?'

'Because I have prayed for thee, that whatever the devil does to you, he will not touch your faith. He cannot touch your faith, Peter, but He is going to sift you tonight. Your faith has got to do with me, as your Saviour'.

Oh, I pray that I may be given the power to overcome this terrible tyrant. There is only one way. There is only one, solitary way. What is it? Christ must be the Lord of your life. If you want to go through this waste, howling wilderness, you must take Christ as the Lord of your life. If you want deliverance from the snare of the devil, because, 'some are taken captive by him at his will', there is only one way and that is, when Christ is the Lord of your life.

Consequently, we must find out from our Bible, what the Lord would have us to do. If I take Him as the Lord of my life, go where He leads and do what He asks; if I do what He commands and go where He sends, then I am delivered from the bondage of the tyrant. That is what Baptism means. That is what I Corinthian's teaching underlines. It underlines the fact that I am taking Christ as the Lord of my life. Can you see that?

If you are not baptised, then when you do obey your Saviour's will, in Baptism, will you remember what you are publicly declaring? Do not worry about the public for the moment. Think about yourself. Do you know what you are stating? You are saying, 'From this very moment, Christ is going to be the Lord of my life.' Is that not beautiful?

There is no happiness, except in obeying Him, every step of the way. Even though the way be hard. He says, 'Take my yoke upon you, learn of me'. I Corinthians is trying to teach us that Baptism has got to do with the taking of Christ as the Lord of my life.

If I were preaching the Gospel here, and someone got saved, and they asked me, 'Will you baptize me?' I would take them to the nearest river, or baptise them in the tank, within five minutes of being saved. Baptism has nothing to do with entrance

Baptism

into the Assembly. It has got to do with entrance to the Kingdom, and that is different.

In the New Testament Scriptures, I read of a man and he was in a chariot. The Gospel was preached to him and he said,

'You know, I believe, May I be baptised?'

'Well, I suppose, if you sit at the back for two or three months, we will see what we can do'.

No, not really.

Philip said, 'Here is water. Only one thing hinders you. Are you a believer?'

'I believe'.

'Let's go down.'

And down into the water they went and the man was baptised. Christ, was the Lord of his life.

Baptism is not disassociated with being saved. Do you know why? Because Christ is my Saviour, that is my sins put away; but now I am baptised – Christ is my Lord. These two go together.

If you take Christ as your Saviour and do not take Him as

your Lord, you are heading for spiritual shipwreck, because the only way to go through this waste, howling wilderness is to accept Christ as the Lord of your life. Could I write over that, that I am telling myself that Christ is forevermore the Lord of my life?

Let us go to I Peter, chapter 3, where it says, 'Whereby Baptism doth also now save us'. What does that mean? How does Baptism save you?

I will tell you an interesting thing. I remember when I was in work and after a while I got some promotion. When something like this happened, then it was the usual thing to take everybody out and stand them a drink, or something, But I did not bother! I did not even buy them a pint of milk. I did not even give them a caramel. I was not built that way. Further, there was no one in the department who expected it. When others got promotion they never invited me. Do you know why? Because they knew I would not go. I took my stand. I never had to refuse! They just knew that they need not ask me because I would not go. The very first time they asked me, I said, "If I went, I would only spoil your fun and you would spoil mine, for we are altogether different; you enjoy yourself and I will enjoy myself

Baptism

in my own way". The very fact that I had taken my stand, saved me. Do you know what I mean? It was not that I was in a quandary whether to go or not. I had already taken my stand and I was not asked again.

Do you know, that is exactly what happened, in the Acts of the Apostles, chapter 2! Here were persons who had willingly, deliberately, taken the Lord Jesus Christ and put the nails through His hands. They said,

'We will not have this Man to reign over us'.

And they nailed him publicly to a tree. Then, they later found that they had made a major mistake and said,

'O Peter, what shall we do? Our sins, our sins, our sins!'

He said, 'What did you do to the Lord of glory? You pinned Him publicly to the tree. Now go and publicly confess your mistake.'

You see, there is a sense that when you are baptised publicly, that it helps you to stand. It breaks the ice. It is telling everyone that you are saved. It is telling everyone that you belong to the Lord Jesus. People will not ask you now, to go to places you used to go to. Do you know why? You have taken Christ as your Saviour. But further, you are baptised: You have taken Christ as your Lord. They may not understand it but they know Who you are associating yourself with and they will not ask you. That is the meaning of I Peter, chapter 3.

Not so very long ago there stood, before me, a young man. Beside him there stood a young lady. Somewhere, I am not so sure exactly where he was, because I was not interested, but there sat a registrar. Indeed, I could hardly tell you whether it was a lady or gentleman, for I was too interested in what was before me. By and by I said to the young man,

"Will you take this young lady to be your lawful wedded wife, to love her, to cherish her, until death do you part?"

"I will."

"And will you take this young man to be your lawful wedded husband, to love, honour and obey him, till death you do part?"

"I will."

Was that the first time they ever said that, or do you think they had it all made up months ago, somewhere? I have a notion they had this all arranged! Indeed, I know, I am married too!

Baptism

I can remember one day, one place, it matters not where, when I said to my girl,

"Adelaide, would you marry me?" Do you know what she said?

"I will."

Why do I have to say it all over again in front of the crowd? Sure, was it not good enough that we had said it in private? The day we were married the good man asked me,

"Rowan Jennings, will you take Adelaid Milne to your lawful wedded wife?"

And I said "I will."

Then he turned around, to my bride and said,

"Adelaid Milne, will you take Rowan Jennings, to be your lawful wedded husband?"

And she said, "I will".

As soon as I said, "I will", and as soon as my bride said, "I will", we were joined in matrimony – but not till then. What happened in private had to be made public. What sort of a conscience would anybody have of living with a young lady without that public confession?

And what is Baptism? It is a public announcement of what

took place in private. Just that. Now I have a clear conscience before God and I am telling the whole world what happened the day I was saved. It does not save you, it is not the washing away of the sins of the flesh, but a clear conscience before God.

Another thing, when these two dear young people stood before me and I asked this one, "Will you?" I asked the question and he answered. Then I asked the young lady, "Will you?" I asked the question and she answered. Did you ever have a little conversation with God? Many a time I did. It is one of the sweetest things I know. Many a time I have raised my heart, in the middle of the night, or even when driving the car, or even when sitting alone in my study and said, "I love you". It is beautiful. Just to have that little welling up within you, "I love you, Lord". God loves you to tell Him that. He just loves it.

When I got married (I will never forget that day, how could I?) I put a ring on my wife's finger. At 2 o'clock on the 12th January, for years, and years, my wife sat on my knee and she pulled the ring off and said, "Here put it on again and tell me you still love me". I had to do what I was told, of course! So, I pushed the ring back on again and said, "I love you just as much as ever I did. Maybe even more". And she went away with a

Baptism

smile on her face, perfectly satisfied for another year. Did you ever realise that God wants you to tell Him that you love Him? I could prove that to you. I could prove that from Hebrews, chapter 6.

In Baptism, God is asking you a question,

"Do you love me?"

"Oh, yes, I do Lord. I am going to show it to You. Watch me go down into those waters of Baptism. I will show You that I love You."

"Were you a sinner?"

"I was indeed, Lord."

"What happened to you?"

"Your Son died for me, Lord."

"Do you agree with me on that?"

"I do indeed. Wait till You see, Lord. Wait till You see the way I agree with You."

Down into the waters of Baptism.

"Did you deserve to get saved?"

"No, I did not, Lord."

"But My Son died for you, did He not?"

"He did indeed."

"He put away all your sins?"

"He did indeed."

"And He did it for nothing, did He not? Do you believe that?"

"I do, Lord, and I am going to show You that I love You for that".

A little talk with God. An asking and an answering of questions, and a clear conscience will help to save you in life. That is the meaning of I Peter, chapter 3.

What could I write over that? It is not God telling me now, but I am telling God. When we turn to the Gospel according to Matthew, it is God telling me, "You go and get baptised." In I Corinthians, chapter 10, I am telling myself, in I Peter, chapter 3, I am telling God. You would not take that from Him, would you?

Chapter 6, of the Roman Epistle, is a different thing still. It is telling the world now. I used to read fairy tale stories when I was a little child. There was one fairy tale about a man called,

Baptism

Sinbad the Sailor. I have often wondered whether the man who wrote the story, about Sinbad the Sailor, studied Romans, chapter 6? I do not know, but the more I used to read it, or think about it, the more I came to the conclusion that he understood Romans, chapter 6. The first thing to notice is that, the sailor was called Sinbad. Now that is very interesting! The second thing, in the particular story that I have in mind, is that he met an old man of the isles, which is also very interesting. An old man. You can read the old man's story in Romans, chapter 6.

In this particular story, of Sinbad and the old man, the old man was sitting by the roadside and he said to Sinbad, one day,

"Sinbad, will you take me on your shoulders and bring me somewhere?"

Sinbad, being a very kindly sort of soul said "Jump up, son". So up the old man went, sat himself on Sinbad's shoulders and wrapped his legs around his neck. Sinbad brought the old man to the cross-roads, in question, and said, "Hop off". But the old man did not, 'hop off', he just stayed there. The result was that instead of Sinbad going where he liked, he had to go where he was told. He had that old man wrapped around his neck day and night, and he could not get rid of him and he directed Sinbad in the way he wanted him to go. When the old man wanted to stop,

Sinbad had to stop. If the old man wanted to sleep, Sinbad had to lie down and sleep. Oh, what a story of Romans, chapter 6.

One day Sinbad got rid of the old man. I am not going to tell you how he got rid of him, the story fails there, but I want to tell you how he could have got rid of him without any difficulty. Suppose that Sinbad had laid down and died! What would have happened? Well, the old man would have disengaged himself. He would have said, "I am out of business here". That is exactly what it says in Romans, chapter 6. Justified, out of business.

"I had better go find another man to wrap my legs around."

Sinbad would have been dead, of course, but what if he had been raised from the dead? He would have been freed, forever, from the old man. Do you know, that is exactly what happens in Romans, chapter 6? That old man in which you were born, that old man called Adam, directing you by a sinful way, directing you by inherent habits – how could you ever be freed from him? Only one way, to die in Christ.

What we find here, in the Epistle to the Romans, is our tell-

Baptism

ing the whole wide world,

"Look at the Lord Jesus, I want you to watch Him. Why was He there, on the cross?"

The world will answer,

"He was a felon."

Did they not nail Him by the hands and feet beside two others? What were they but robbers and thieves? Why was the Lord in the midst? Because He was also crucified as a felon. What did He say? Nothing. What do you want to tell the world, in Romans, chapter 6? I am going to tell the whole wide world that, that Man, who died on the middle cross, did not die for his own sins, but for mine. I was a felon. He died for me and I have now died in Him. Therefore, I am rid of the old man.

Mind you, if you were going to die and be buried, and if this act, of Romans, chapter 6, is going to be carried out in your life, do not think that you have to wait till you are good enough. There is only one thing good for a dead man and that is the grave. The reason why the man died, in Romans, chapter 6, was because he was bad and God will have no contact with that old man. Therefore, I declare to the whole wide world that I have died in Him.

Church Principles for Today

Finally, I am very happy to report that they did not keep me under the water! In chapter 2, I told you of my experience with the great big man who wanted to be baptised. According to Archimedes principle, it would have been all right, if the tank had been well filled and not been so leaky! He would have floated and I would have had no trouble! But by the time the meeting was over, and I was ready to baptise the man, there was hardly enough to cover him. When I stooped over to put him in, I declare, the two of us nearly went in! If I had not put my hand forward I would have gone into the tank with him! I just got him buried and no more. But he did go down and I am glad to say that I had enough strength to get him up.

That is what happens in Romans, chapter 6. You come up again declaring that you now have a new life. With a new life - not a changed life. The old man is dead. You come up symbolically declaring that when God saved you, you received something you never had before. What do you think of that now?

God did not change your character, He gave you a new one. He did not change your nature, He gave you a new one. All that you used to be, God buried it out of His sight and brought you up and gave you a nature, and a life like, unto His Son.

Baptism

Do you agree with God? "I am fit for nothing, only the grave, Lord. I am going to show it to you." Down into the water I go. That is Romans, chapter 6.

In conclusion, therefore, I have taken Christ as my Saviour and my God, and He has delivered me from the power of an evil prince. As God, He has commanded that I obey Him, in Baptism, as we read in Matthew, chapter 28 and I remind myself of this fact, in I Corinthians, chapter 10.

According to I Peter, chapter 3, I am publicly announcing my relationship to Him and that I love Him. And, in Romans, chapter 6, I am confessing that I was a sinner, but He made me a new man.

So in a word, I am telling the world that I am a new man in Christ. Beautiful!

Chapter 6

The Lord's Supper

Our reading, for this chapter, will be found in:

I Corinthians, chapter 11, verses 23 - 34:

"For I have received of the Lord that which also I delivered unto you, That the Lord Jesus the same night in which he was betrayed took bread: And when he had given thanks, he brake it, and said, Take, eat: this is my body, which is broken for you: this do in remembrance of me."

(Now, the dear saints will appreciate that the word 'broken', in verse 24, is not in the original script. The Lord Jesus Christ's body was not broken. It may have been pierced but nowhere, in the Scriptures, is there a hint of the body of the Lord Jesus being broken. And because we break the bread, it does not mean that it symbolises a body which was broken. That is not so. So this word, 'broken', is not here).

So from verse 24 it should read:

"And when he had given thanks, he brake it, and said, Take, eat: This is my body, which is for you: This do in remembrance of me. After the same manner also he took the cup, when he had supped".

(Now, we have no Scripture to substantiate if the Lord Jesus actually took the cup Himself. It does not really say. If you look at your Revised Version again, you will find that, 'after He had supped' is really, 'after the supper'. So what really happened was that after the Passover Supper was over, the Lord Jesus instituted this feast. If we bear this in mind, it will help us not to fall into some particular avenues which are not in I Corinthians, chapter 11, at all.)

So again, from verse 25, it reads:

"After the same manner also he took the cup, after supper, saying, This cup is the new testament (the new covenant) in my blood: this do ye, as oft as ye drink it, in remembrance of me. For as often as ye eat this bread, and drink this cup, ye do show the Lord's death till he come. Wherefore whosoever shall eat this bread, and drink this cup of the Lord, unworthily, shall be guilty of the body and blood of the Lord. But let a man examine himself and so let him eat of that bread, and drink of that cup. For he that eateth and drinketh unworthily, eateth and drinketh judgment, (not damnation) to himself, not discerning the Lord's body. For this cause many are weak and sickly among you, and many sleep. For if we would judge ourselves, we should not be judged. But when we are judged, we are chastened of the Lord, that we should not be condemned with the world. Wherefore, my brethren, when ye come together to eat, tarry one for another. And if any man hunger, let him eat at home; that ye come not together unto condemnation (or judgment). And the rest will I set in order when I come."

Church Principles for Today

Mr. David Craig's Outline

Many of us come together, every Lord's Day morning, to break the bread and drink the cup, in memory of our Lord. We have come to the conclusion, honestly, have we not, that the only purpose of the Breaking of Bread meeting is to remember the Lord? But I would ask you a question at the beginning of this chapter. In what way should we remember Him? Now, I want to answer that.

I remember many, many years ago, I used to go to visit the late Mr. David Craig. I had very happy moments with him. One night when I was visiting him, he gave me a little outline of the Lord's Supper, which was very sweet. As he was talking to me, I wrote it into the margin of my Bible and I want to go over what he said. You will appreciate, that what he said was altogether, and absolutely, true.

He said, "The Lord's Supper is an ordinance." You know, he was right.

In the last chapter we were speaking of Baptism and we saw that Baptism was an Ordinance. As we showed there are only

The Lord's Supper

two ordinances in the New Testament: The Ordinance of Baptism and the Ordinance of the Lord's Supper. There are no others. We find that both these ordinances were instituted by the Person of the Lord Jesus in the Gospels. Both these ordinances were practised by the disciples, in the Acts of the Apostles. Both of them are explained, and taught, to us in the Epistles. If you want to learn anything about the reasons for these ordinances then you need not go to the Gospels, nor do you need to go to the Acts of the Apostles, but what you must do, is to go to the Epistles.

Mr. Craig said, 'It is an Ordinance,' and so it is. Instituted by the Lord Jesus, but not in the Gospel of Matthew; instituted by the Lord Jesus, but not in the Gospel by Mark; instituted by the Lord Jesus in the Gospel according to Luke, for only in that Gospel does the Lord Jesus say, "This do in remembrance of me." It is an Ordinance. The teaching of that Ordinance is given to us in I Corinthians, chapter 11. Mr. Craig was right.

Said Mr. Craig, "Brother Jennings, it is a remembrance." And he was right. It says it, "This do in remembrance of me." I want to deal with that more fully, in fact, the burden of this chapter is around those words. What does it mean when it says,

"This do in remembrance of me"?

Sometimes when my beloved brethren, (now I am not finding fault) stand up in the Remembrance Meeting and pray, "We are so happy, Lord, to be here this morning, and to get away from the cares of life." As soon as they say that, my mind jumps to the cares of life. As soon as they say, "To guide us away from the problems of life", the very first thing that comes to mind are all the problems of the week. We would like to be positive, would we not, and forget about the problems of the week and come together, for one hour, to be lifted up into that Mountain to remember Him? Mr. Craig was right, it is a remembrance.

Said Mr. Craig, "You know, brother, the Morning Meeting is a declaration". And it is. 'This do, and as ye do it, ye declare.' I wonder what it means when it says "You declare the Lord's death"? In what way do you declare the Lord's death? I am going to explain that to you.

Then he said, "It is a fellowship." For we all gather around the one table and we all partake of the same loaf. And the fact that you partake of that loaf, and I partake of the same loaf, constitutes you and me being in fellowship. We are in fellowship

The Lord's Supper

one with the other because we both partake of the same loaf.

It is, therefore, a complete contradiction for me to take that loaf with you and not to be in fellowship with you. There is something wrong. If I were to sit down with you in the Morning Meeting and break that bread and then not shake hands with you as you went through the door, there is something terribly wrong! It is a complete contradiction in terms. So it is a fellowship when we gather together to remember Him. Mr. Craig was right.

I remember, just after the war, a Christian returned home after travelling on the Continent. He had come across a little group of Christians gathered together, in lovely terms, somewhere in France, and he gathered with them. By and by, the day came for the Breaking of Bread. Someone gave thanks for the bread and eventually it was handed to him. He took his piece and was waiting patiently on someone giving thanks for the cup, but there was a long, long time and no thanks was given. He eventually got a nudge, and he looked to find the loaf was there again. He passed no remark, took another piece and handed it on to the next person. He waited patiently, again, for someone to give thanks for the cup, but no thanks came. Eventually, he got yet another nudge with an elbow, and here was the loaf again! What actually happened was that the loaf went round, and round, and round, till there was no loaf left. Oh, I can see the point. What once was one loaf, was divided equally amongst all the members, and now the one loaf was in them – they were one fellowship.

A couple of years later he went back, and there they were still breaking bread, but the loaf went round just once. In the couple of years between, they had changed, but the point was that it was a fellowship.

Said Mr. Craig, "Brother Jennings, it is a prospect. Does it not state, so clearly, in I Corinthians, chapter 11, verse 26, '... till he come'?"

We are all looking forward to the coming of the Lord Jesus. Some of these mornings we will break the bread for the very last time. It will not be the last time because you are going to pass through death to be with the Lord, but because the Lord Jesus Christ is going to come. Oh, beautiful, 'prospect'.

The Lord's Supper

Then, Mr. Craig said, "It is a retrospect". You see, we look back to that night in which He was betrayed. Our minds go away back, and sometimes, in the eyes of our imagination, we can see Him in the Upper Room with all the disciples gathered around Him. We can almost hear the words that fell from His lips, "With desire I have desired to eat this Passover with you before I suffer." Then after that He took the bread. We look back and we can almost see Him, with John leaning on His breast as they reclined at the table, and had that first remembrance meeting, if we can call it that.

Then not only that, "It is a discernment." This is a hard word to understand. What does it mean to discern the Lord's body? Now I trust you will be able to understand that before the end of the chapter.

Then after that he said, "It is a commandment." We are going to look at that also, and see, indeed, that it is an obligation. You are commanded to come and break this bread. It is not, 'Will you?' It is not a request. It is an obligation, in fact, it is a downright order.

I trust, that when we go on holiday, we go to a place where

we can remember the Lord. I trust, we never try to get a holiday from the Lord, but rather seek to find the nearest little Assembly and gather there to remember the Lord Jesus. Said Mr. Craig, "It is a commandment."

I think those are beautiful things. There are eight of them. See Table 6.1.

>   Ordinance
>   Remembrance
>   Declaration
>   Fellowship
>   Prospect
>   Retrospect
>   Discernment
>   Commandment

Table 6.1: **Mr. D. Craigs' outline of the Lord's Supper**

Those thoughts that Mr. Craig gave me, so many years ago, have remained right at the front of my mind ever since, for they were absolutely correct.

The Old and New Covenants

However, I want to point out another aspect, on top of the

The Lord's Supper

above eight. An entirely different aspect that lies right on the very surface of our Bibles. Indeed, it was not until someone pointed it out to me, a few years ago, that I may honestly declare, I ever noticed it myself. Perhaps I was dull of learning. It was there all the time but I just had not noticed it.

Let us forget about the Lord's Supper for a moment or two. We will come back to it but let us start on a new tack.

I am sure you have heard of the New Covenant. I remember the night I was saved, I did not know that this Bible was divided into two parts: The Old Testament and the New, or if you like, the Old Covenant and the New.

Now, the terms of that Old Covenant are found in the Book of Exodus, chapter 20. The terms of the New Covenant are found in the Epistle to the Hebrews, chapters 8 and 10. An Old Covenant and a New Covenant.

Now that Old Covenant was given for two reasons; the New Covenant was also given for two reasons. One of the reasons why the Old Covenant was given, was that it might be a legal agreement between God and man. So also with the New. Further, the Old Covenant was a means whereby God ordered the life of His people. And so with the New.

I want to say a little more about the Covenants. Their study, of course, would take chapters, if not books, but all I want to do is to introduce you to that which is called the, 'New Covenant', which most saints will have heard of.

When we sometimes preach the Gospel, we quote, "Your sins and iniquities I will remember no more". What we are doing is, we are preaching one of the terms of the New Covenant. "Your sins and your iniquities I will remember no more" – and we revel in that. But remember, that is only one of the terms of the New Covenant! Just one. Sometimes we are so taken up with this particular element that we forget that there is another. The preachers of the Gospel lay all the stress of their being on the fact that our sins and our iniquities are remembered no more. That is what we talk about when we think of Christ as our Saviour.

But listen to the other term, "I will put my laws into their hearts and in their minds will I write them". Mind you, this sec-

The Lord's Supper

ond term is the way God wishes to govern your life.

He is going to save you, but he also wants to govern you. In a word: Christ is your Saviour ("Your sins and iniquities I will remember no more"), but Christ is your Lord ('In your hearts I will write my laws'). These two go together and, 'what the Lord has put together, let not man pull asunder'.

I want to draw a simple sketch for you, in order to clarify this more fully. One of the first things I will draw is just simply three circles. Then, I am going to write something in each of them. There does not seem to be much sense in this, but we are going to see how the Morning Meeting and the New Covenant are vitally connected.

In one of the circles I am going to write, 'New Covenant'. Then, I am going to write, into the second circle, 'Christ is Lord'. You can see, from Figure 6.1 that Christ as the Lord of my life and the New Covenant are indissolubly linked. The two circles are intertwined! No one can deny that. It is so plain. Christ, as the Lord of my life, is an element of salvation which must be taken with Christ, as my Saviour. These two go together and they must not be separated.

Church Principles for Today

Now I know that my friends, the evangelists, emphasise that first one. But I am going to suggest to you that the second one, Christ as the Lord of my life, is altogether neglected. I am going to emphasise that, as I talk about the Lord's Supper.

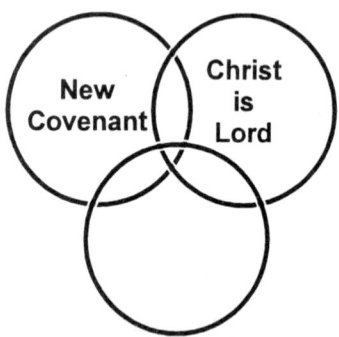

Figure 6.1: The New Covenant relationship to The Headship of Christ

If we were to turn to Romans, chapter 10, verse 9, we would read, "If thou shalt confess with thy mouth 'Jesus as thy **Lord**' ... thou shalt be saved." That is what it says. We have referred in chapter 6, that the very first words Paul spoke, in the Acts of the Apostles, chapter 9, after he was saved were, "**Lord**, what wilt thou have me to do?" We also reminded ourselves that the thief hanging on the cross, beside the Lord Jesus, in the Gospel according to Luke, chapter 23, said, '**Lord**, remember me'. Do you realise that the Lord Jesus is the Lord of your life? Hence, the first point that I can see so very, very clearly, is that the New Covenant and Christ as the Lord of my life are indissolubly re-

The Lord's Supper

lated and it would save us a lot of trouble if we appreciated that and put it into practice.

Now, having seen that, let us turn to the Gospel according to Matthew, chapter 26, verses 27 and 28. Here is what we learn, "And he (the Lord Jesus) took the cup, and gave thanks, and gave it to them saying, Drink ye all of it; For this is my blood of the new testament (Covenant) which is shed for many for the remission of sins." What do you think Matthew is trying to tell us? He is seeking to show us that the Supper and the New Covenant are also linked. See Figure 6.2.

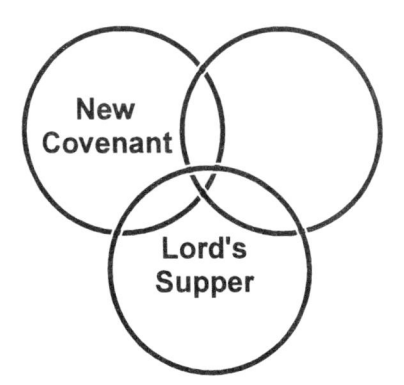

Figure 6.2: The New Covenant's relationship to the Lord's Supper.

If we were to turn to the Gospel according to Mark, chapter 14, verses 23 and 24, we would read these words, "And he took the cup, and when he had given thanks, he gave it to them: and they all drank of it. And he said unto them, This is my blood of the new testament (Covenant), which is shed for many." Again, the New Covenant and the Lord's Supper are linked.

If we were to take the institution of the Supper, in Luke, we would read in chapter 22, verse 20, "Likewise also the cup after supper, saying, This cup is the new testament (Covenant) in my blood ..." The Lord Jesus again unites the New Covenant with the Supper.

Further, we quoted at the beginning of this chapter, I Corinthians, chapter 11. Verse 25 reads, "This cup is the new testament (Covenant) in my blood".

Now I believe you are intelligent. Could you, firstly deny that there is a relationship between the New Covenant and Christ, as the Lord of my life? No, you would agree with that. Could you deny that this New Covenant has got to do with, "my laws I will put in your heart and in your mind I will write them"? No, you would agree with that, also. Why? That He might direct my life. The New Covenant and Christ as the Lord of my life are indissolubly related.

The Lord's Supper

But secondly, we have proved, conclusively, from Matthew, Mark, Luke and I Corinthians, that the New Covenant and the Lord's Supper are also indissolubly related.

Now, a question. Is it possible that the Lord's Supper is indissolubly related to Christ, as the Lord of my life? Now I have got to prove that. If I can prove it, I am going to suggest that, this is an aspect of the Lord's Supper which is largely overlooked. See Figure 6.3.

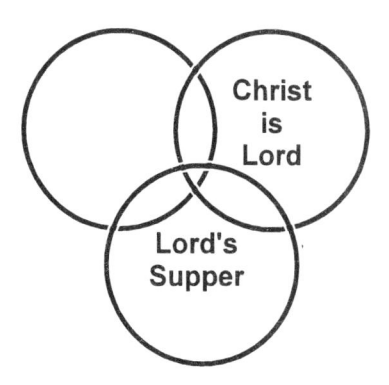

Figure 6.3:   **The Lordship of Christ**

We read in I Corinthians, chapter 11, verse 23, "I have received of the Lord that which also I delivered unto you." Now I want to ask another question. From whom did Paul receive this message? He received it from the, 'Saviour of men'. That is not what it says. Oh, he received it from, 'the Lamb'. It does not say that either. Well, he must have received it from, 'the Redeemer'. It does not say that either! What it does say is, "I have received of, 'the Lord'". We have hardly started to read the passage until Christ, as Lord, is related to the Supper.

Look at verse 23 again, "The Lord Jesus that night in which He was betrayed". You would have thought that should have been, 'the Saviour', would you not? Surely, it should have read, 'The Saviour on the night in which He was betrayed ...'. But it does not. Nor is it, 'the Lamb'; nor is it, 'the Redeemer'; nor any of those beautiful titles that are given to the Lord Jesus, with reference to His sacrifice. What it does say is, "The Lord Jesus that night in which He was betrayed." So, before you come out of the very first verse, the title of, 'Lord' is mentioned twice, with reference to the Supper.

Look at verse 26, of I Corinthians, chapter 11. Notice what it says there, "For as often as ye eat this bread, and drink this cup, ye do shew the ..." Who's death? " ... the Lord's death ...". Now why does it say, 'the Lord's death'?

I am going to explain that to you but, first of all, can you not

The Lord's Supper

see that here, in I Corinthians, chapter 11, where we are given the doctrine and teaching of the Lord's Supper, that the Lordship of Christ is indissolubly related to that Supper?

Notice again what it says in verse 27, "Wherefore whosoever shall eat this bread, and drink this cup of 'the Lord', unworthily, shall be guilty of the body and blood of 'the Lord'."

Notice what it says in verse 29, "For he that eateth and drinketh unworthily, eateth and drinketh judgment to himself, not discerning 'the Lord's' body."

Notice what it says in verse 32, "But when we are judged, we are chastened of 'the Lord'..." Can you see that I Corinthians, chapter 11, is setting before us the beautiful truth that the Lord's Supper and Christ, as the Lord of my life, are indissolubly related?

"Oh", says somebody, "Titles do not mean anything". Well then, read the first half of I Corinthians, chapter 11, and there you will find Christ is not presented as the Lord, at all. There He is presented as the Head. The chapter suddenly breaks and instead of looking upon Christ as the Head it suddenly begins to talk about Christ as Lord. Why the change, if titles do not mean anything?

So we find here, on the very surface of this chapter, the Lord's death, the Lord's Supper, and Christ as Lord, indissolubly related. See Figure 6.4.

Now let us look at these verses again. Verse 23 says, "the night in which he was betrayed". Why does it say that? Why should the Lord's Supper begin to talk about the night in which He was betrayed? Tell me, what happened that night? Who betrayed Him? A man, called Judas Iscariot. He sold Him for thirty pieces of silver. Why did he sell Him? Because he said in his heart, 'I will not have this man to reign over me'. In other words, we find buried in the chapter, a man who refused to accept Christ as the Lord of his life. What did he do? He got rid of Him by selling Him. Is that why it says here, "the night in which he was betrayed"? Here was a man who would not have Christ to reign over him and he got Him put to death.

Notice what it says in verse 26. "The Lord's death..." Why does it speak about the Lord's death? What happened then? A

The Lord's Supper

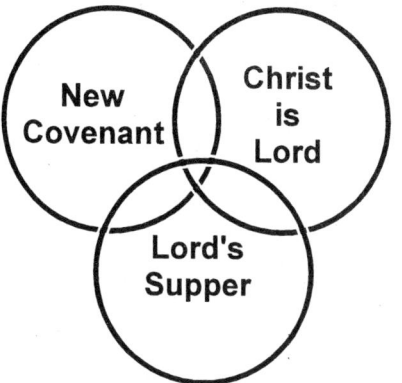

Figure 6.4: **The Remembrance Supper**

great crowd of people gathered around Pilot's rostrum and they said, 'Give us Barabbas, but crucify this King'. Or, if you prefer to use the words of the parable, that crowd said, 'We will not have this Man to reign over us'. They did not want Christ as Lord. So again, buried in the chapter, I do not only see a man who would not accept Christ as Lord of his life, but I see a group of people, indeed, a nation, which said, 'We will not have Christ as the Lord of our lives'.

Notice verse 26 again, "Till He come". What will happen when He comes? The Scripture makes it perfectly plain what will happen. Let me read it to you. Psalm 2, verse 9, "Thou shalt break them with a rod of iron; thou shalt dash them in pieces like a potter's vessel." What is going to happen when the

Lord comes? He will not ask them then, 'Will you accept Me, with your heart, as the Lord of your life'. He will be the Lord and He will dash them in pieces as one would dash a potter's vessel. That is what is going to happen when He comes.

Notice what it says in Psalm 2, verse 6, "Yet have I set my King upon my holy hill of Zion." That is what is going to happen when He comes, and nobody on this Earth will say then, 'We will not have this Man to reign over us' Why? For God is going to set Him upon His holy hill, as King and Lord.

Now, what is happening between that night in which He was betrayed and the day in which He will come? Little companies of believers are gathered all over the world and what do they say? They say, 'We **will** have this Man to reign over us'.

Is that not what you said the night you were saved? "For if thou shalt confess with thy mouth, 'Jesus as thy Lord', thou shalt be saved" (Romans, chapter 10, verse 9). The Lord of my life!

Do you see the point? If you partake of that Supper, you are acknowledging every time you do, that Christ is the Lord of

The Lord's Supper

your life. Now tell me. Is He? Or would you have the utter audacity to actually partake of the Supper and not to do what He tells you? You would not do that, would you?

You beloved brethren, the last thing I would want to do is to tread on your toes and if I would hurt a soul I would not be able to sleep. My wife can testify to that. But let me ask you a simple question. Is there anything in your life that the Lord has asked you to do and you will not do it, and yet you take the Supper? Beloved sisters in Christ, you know I would not hurt you, I want to help you. Do you know of anything that the Lord would love you to do? Would you say to Him, "I will not have You to reign over me"? Would you?

When you take of the Supper you are saying, 'Christ is the Lord of my life'. Is that not a declaration? Can you see the declaration now, perfectly clearly? When I take that Supper, I am declaring that Christ is the Lord of my life.

I know of many a Sunday morning, when the brethren would bring you to tears. I know that and I love it, too. There is nothing so sweet to remember the Person of our Lord Jesus, in His sufferings: To think of His wounds; to think of His love; to think of the hours of darkness; to think of His form. But it says, 'To discern the Lord's body.' That means to think. Apart from all the sanctimonious beauty, do not forget that at the very core, at the very centre, of the Lord's Supper you are declaring that Christ is the Lord of your life.

Would you dare to say to the Lord after the meeting is over, or even as you take the bread, 'I will not have this Man to reign over me'. Watch you do not drop dead. Watch it!

The Lord said, "This do". This do? That is a commandment. From whom? The Lord of my life! Therefore, it will not be a matter of, 'I am tired this morning. I will just not go!' Oh, I know all about the little children. I know all about that. We had little children, also. Too young to sit at the back. We had to take it week about. There was no alternative. The Lord understands that. I know that there are certain duties that have to be performed that prevent the brethren and sisters from coming out to the Lord's Day Morning Meeting. But would you ask yourself this question next Sunday morning? 'He commands me to go to the meeting, this morning. Now, shall I go? Remember, He is the Lord of your life.

The Lord's Supper

Now, if you do not obey Him, I am going to tell you what happens, according to I Corinthians, chapter 11.

May I say it again: When I am on holidays, do I still hear that command ringing in my ears, "This do"? Or does laziness, or excitement, overcome me? God forbid that I gallivant when the brethren are sitting down to partake of this Supper.

Sisters, brethren, do you know what I am telling you? I am telling you that the Morning Meeting is a place of judgment! Now, do not throw my argument out just yet! I am saying that the Morning Meeting is a place of judgment, because I am declaring, when I break that bread and drink that cup, that Christ is the Lord of my life. But then let me ask myself the question, "Is He?" Where would you get that in I Corinthians, chapter 11? Read verse 28, and see exactly what it says, "But let a man examine himself". Can you understand that now? "Let a man examine himself, and so let him eat".

I would be foolish to pretend that I am perfect; far, far be such a thought from my words. But would it be all right if I did say to you, that every Lord's Day morning, when I break that bread, one thought crosses my mind; "Is there any sphere in my life where Christ is not my Lord?" And then I eat. Is that what is here? Yes. Would it not be an awful thing to remember the sufferings of Christ, and then to deny Him His rightful place in your life? It says perfectly clearly, "Let a man examine himself". What is it? The Supper, indissolubly linked, with Christ as the Lord of my life.

Look what it says in verse 29, "Discern the Lord's body". What does that mean? Would it be all right if I just translated that as, "Think, consider your life"? Is He the Lord of my life, or am I down-right denying His precepts, as clearly set out in the Word of God?

Now, if I know what He wants me to do and will not do it, then there is a sphere of my life in which He is not the Lord, and if this Supper is going to be a place of judgment, it would be far better for me if I stayed at home. However, we must remember the very first command of I Corinthians, chapter 11 was, "This do". So I cannot stay at home! I dare not! Do you know why? Because He is the Lord of my life and He says, 'Go'. So I have got to go. Now that I am there, I have got to ask myself the question, 'Is He the Lord of my life, in all spheres?'

The Lord's Supper

Is there a sense that the Lord Jesus knows that we are very forgetful people and, between the hustle and bustle of work and the responsibilities of home, I forget that He is the Lord of my life? I wonder what would happen to your Assembly, if every single brother and sister, next Sunday morning, as they broke that bread, said with an open heart to the Lord, "Lord, is there any sphere in my life where You are not my Lord?" There would be a revival! In all events, the branches would go over the wall and that would be the end of all problems, if there are any.

When I read I Corinthians, chapter 11, I find that the Lord is very gracious. He permits the first act of judgment to be by me. He says, 'You judge yourself'. So, He is not going to judge you, at least, not yet. He wants you to do it. So I come together with the beloved saints to break that bread and rejoice, and revel, in all the beauties which the brethren bring before me; and I think of dear Mr. Craig, with his ordinance, and his remembrance, and his declaration, and his fellowship, and his prospect, and his retrospect, and discernment and the commandment. I revel in it all, and then I break the bread and ask myself the question, "Is He the Lord of my life?" If He is not, then what do I do? If He is not the Lord of your life and you take the emblems, do you know what is happening? 'You are eating and drinking judgment to yourself!' Could words be any more plain? You are actually eating and drinking judgment on yourself!

Has the Lord changed any? We will deal more with this when we come to Assembly Discipline, in chapter 7, and we will learn that the last thing the Lord wants to do is to discipline you. That is why He hands it over to you, first of all, and asks you to examine yourself and if you find no sphere in your life where He is not your Lord, eat. But if you find a sphere and you know that you have disobeyed Him, yet you still say, "I will not", you are eating and drinking judgment to yourself. Why? You are not discerning that it is the Lord you are dealing with. So the first act of judgment is with me.

Is this the reason why we come every week? Is this the reason why it says, 'As oft as you come'? Suppose we only broke the bread once a year. Can you show me, in the Scripture, where it says we must break it every Lord's Day? I could. You could too. Mind you, I am going far beyond the Acts of the Apostles, chapter 20. Why not once a year? A whole 364 days fall in between and by the end of the year I have forgotten alto-

The Lord's Supper

gether that Christ is the Lord of my life ... as often as I do it, I must remind my heart ... indeed, day-by-day, I must remind my heart, and if I do not, then when I gather together on Sunday morning, I will remember it then.

So, is He the Lord of my life? Well, I will have to examine my heart. Then, I find that He is not found in every sphere – so I will stay away. But I must come, because He, as the Lord of my life, commands it. Then I will come. But I know very well that there are things that I should do and I am not doing them. Right! 'He that eateth and drinketh unworthily shall be guilty ....'

How could I be eating and drinking unworthily? How do I know that Christ is the Lord of my life? I will tell you in a word. Luke, chapter 6, verse 46, "Why call me, Lord, Lord, and do not the things that I say?"

When we come together, on the Lord's Day morning, I ask myself this question, "Is He the Lord of my life?" If we would judge ourselves, says verse 31, 'We should not be judged'.

So, I repeat, God gives the first judgment to me but if I do not obey, then He will come in and do it. Trials come into our life, says I Corinthians, chapter 10, because we are human beings. But it is God's desire that you should judge your life, to look at your life, and when things are not going too sweetly, then ask yourself this question, "Is it possible that this is the rod of the Lord?" Because Hebrews, chapter 12, makes it perfectly plain that He does chastise His children.

If you have never received chastisement from the Lord, I am sorry, you are not saved! I am not saying that, I am quoting to you from Hebrews, chapter 12.

Oh, if you examine your life you will see His rod. Perhaps, if an Assembly would examine its life it would see the rod too. Maybe that is why, at times, there is not the peace, and love, and fellowship, and harmony and success!

Would it be a lovely thing to go to I Corinthians, chapter 11, and then to go into Matthew, Mark, Luke and John (Oh, I know the Supper is not in John, but it is not hard to show where it fitted in) and to find that from the very context, after the Breaking of Bread comes the exercise of the Gifts? I wonder why that is? It is God's will that when the Supper is over, that the Gifts are

The Lord's Supper

then exercised. What for?

Perhaps I carry things too far, in my way of thinking, but I am going to suggest to you that what the Scripture seems to teach is that when you have partaken of the Lord's Supper, and you have examined your life in the sight and in the presence of your Lord, and discerned that He is the Lord of your life, and you find no avenue, or sphere in your life, where He is not Lord, then you listen with both your ears to the ministry. What are you listening for? To tickle your ears and to go out and say, "That was a good word"? Those things are beautiful, I do the same! But if I am right, what do you listen for, after the Breaking of Bread, when the brother gets up to minister? You listen to see whether the Lord will reveal to you another little sphere in your life that you have not thought of before, where He is not your Lord. Can you see it? It is all so beautiful.

So, it is clear that this Remembrance Meeting has a distinct order which must not be upset. The first thing that we must do is to break the bread. After that, we have to take the cup. Then there is ministry of the Word. Finally, there is the laying aside as the Lord has prospered us. (This will be dealt with in chapter 9.) That is divine order.

Church Principles for Today

This Breaking of Bread service, with its order, was designed that we might remember two things: That we might remember first of all, "This is my body which is given for you" (I Corinthians, chapter 22, verse 24). What a lovely thing! What a lovely search it would be, and how it would warm our hearts, to look through the Old and New Testaments and to notice what God has brought to our attention in the giving of the body of Christ. We would read, "All my bones are out of joint" (Psalm 22, verse 14). We would notice, "I gave my back to the smiters (Isaiah, chapter 50, verse 6) and many other portions so precious to us, all indicating this fact. The next time you take the bread in the Morning Meeting, will you remember that it speaks of the Lord Jesus coming out to you? Coming out to give to you all that He had: "This is my body which is given for you." What a lovely thing for our heart's meditation. Not only to enjoy those audible prayers; not only to enjoy the ministry of His Word; not only to enjoy those lovely hymns that we sing but, in our heart, and mind, to meditate on the very giving of Himself. Hebrews, chapter 10, is a chapter that is set aside for this very purpose – to show us the giving of His body. That is why the bread comes first. He is coming out to give you all He had. Then after that comes the cup.

The Lord's Supper

We have found that it was given to us in Matthew, Mark, Luke and in I Corinthians, chapter 11. Mark never mentions sins connected with that meeting; Luke never mentions sins connected with that meeting; I Corinthians never mentions sins connected with it either; it is only Matthew. Yet, there is something that is common to all four: Not only is the bread mentioned in all four; not only is the cup mentioned in all four; but something else: The covenant. So that God would have us remember, not only His coming out to me and giving all that He had, but also the covenant, and that covenant is our going out to Him.

Now, I would not want to divide this Remembrance Meeting into two. It would be a silly thing to say that up until a certain moment, we should remember the Lord and His coming to me, then for next bit of the meeting we should remember our going to Him. I did not say anything so foolish. What I am saying is that the bread comes first: The Lord Jesus coming out to me and giving me all that He has. But do not forget the cup of the covenant and that covenant is, "I will put my laws in their hearts" (Hebrews, chapter 8, verse 10).

Now look at the order. That bread, His coming out to me and

249

giving all that He had. When He gives that bread it is as if He were saying, 'Look what I gave for thee'. Then when we take the cup He says, 'Now I want you'. So when we take the cup we are saying, 'Yes, I am a member of that covenant. What Lord, must I do now to be holy?' Then after that the ministry. Our prayer then, is that God would feed us; that God would lead us into His truth, that the ministering brethren might feed His children, that they might be channels for others so that they might see something more of the way that God wants to lead them in the paths of holiness of character.

I leave it for your prayerful consideration, with a story. I preach the Gospel nearly every Sunday, but I do not like series of Gospel meetings. I had two of them in my life. Half-way through the first week, in one of them, I took sick. After four or five weeks of the second one I ended up in hospital. The doctors examined me in the Royal Victoria Hospital, Belfast, and they put me in the Intensive Care Unit for a while. I knew only too well what was wrong. If they had asked me I would have told them! "I am having a series of Gospel meetings! That is what is wrong". You see, I took a pain in the back of my neck and I had to stand up to swallow. When I went into hospital they started to look around my chest and I told them that the

The Lord's Supper

pain was not there. They said, "We are not interested in your neck, we are interested in your heart." But the pain was not down at my heart, it was up at my neck, and the reason why it was up there, I will suggest to you, was because of the Gospel meetings! So you can see why I would be very, very slow to take another series.

But I did take the first series, in Scotland. I was over for a conference, when the brethren asked me to stay for a week to preach the Gospel. There was an evangelist with me and the two of us began to preach – and I took sick on the first Wednesday, with a pain in my shoulder. It was like a toothache and I could not lie this way, or that way. I could get no peace, or ease, day or night, until I was going to the plane. On the way to the plane it all went away and never came back!

The first night of those Gospel meetings there was a whole seat of Scots boys and girls, and they had great fun! Not being a gospeler, I hoped they would not come back! That was wrong and I know it was wrong. There you are, I am not a Gospel preacher. But what do you think happened the next night? They all came back. The whole lot of them. They filled the whole seat but they were not just so rowdy. The next night they all came back again and one of the lads stayed behind. He said, "Sirs, I need to be saved." He said, "I am this and I am that. I deal in drugs and I do ...". It does not matter what all he did. He said, "I love it, but I want to get saved. Tell me, Sirs, can I get saved tonight and continue with my drink, continue with my sin, continue with my drugs, can I continue to do what I am doing and get your Saviour?"

What would you have said? Would it be all right if I told you what we said? "Son, if thou shalt confess with thy heart Jesus as thy Lord, thou shalt be saved" (Romans, chapter 10, verse 9). I did not have to tell him anymore. He saw it clearly, he went out and never came back. He would have freely, gladly, taken Christ to do away with the penalty of all his sins and continue with them. But to take Christ as his Saviour and Christ as the Lord of his life, no, he would not have it. But you are not like that!

Chapter 7

Assembly Discipline

In all my days of Christian experience I have never heard anyone minister on Assembly Discipline. Nevertheless, it is an exceedingly important subject and so I trust that the Lord might give you the grace to read patiently and to learn what He, Himself, would say to you.

We shall read then in:

I Corinthians, chapter 5, verses 1 - 13:

"It is reported commonly that there is fornication among

you, and such fornication as is not so much as named among the Gentiles, that one should have his father's wife. And ye are puffed up, and have not rather mourned, that he that hath done this deed might be taken away from among you. For I verily, as absent in body, but present in spirit, have judged already, as though I were present, concerning him that hath so done this deed, In the name of our Lord Jesus Christ, when ye are gathered together, and my spirit, with the power of our Lord Jesus Christ, To deliver such an one unto Satan for the destruction of the flesh, that the spirit may be saved in the day of the Lord Jesus. Your glorying is not good. Know ye not that a little leaven leaveneth the whole lump? Purge out therefore the old leaven, that ye may be a new lump, as ye are unleavened. For even Christ our passover is sacrificed for us: Therefore let us keep the feast, not with old leaven, neither with the leaven of malice and wickedness; but with the unleavened bread of sincerity and truth. I wrote unto you in an epistle not to company with fornicators: Yet not altogether with the fornicators of this world, or with the covetous, or extortioners, or with idolaters; for then must ye needs go out of the world. But now I have written unto you not to keep company, if any man that is called a brother be a fornicator, or covetous, or an idolater, or a railer, or a drunkard, or an extortioner; with such an one no not to eat. For what

Assembly Discipline

have I to do to judge them also that are without? do not ye judge them that are within? But them that are without God judgeth. Therefore put away from among yourselves that wicked person."

The Introduction

We have studied, in chapter 2, the Church – that great, vast company of saved people, from the Day of Pentecost until the coming of the Lord Jesus Christ to the air. We saw that there are many metaphors that were given to that great company, so that we could understand it. Then, we saw that there was another Church – a Local Church – the company of people gathered together here, and there, in the various localities around the world. These small, local gatherings were given similar metaphors to the ones representing the saved of all ages.

One of those was a Temple. The very fact that the 'little thing' is called a Temple, shows that God expects it to be holy. In fact, God does more than expect it to be holy, He demands it to be holy. Indeed, if we were to read, in I Corinthians, chapter 3, we would read this amazing verse, 'if any of you defile the local testimony, him I will defile' (verse 17). So it is a very,

very serious thing to be a member of a Church because there is the possibility that you could bring into it something which would defile its holiness. God has made a promise, He says, 'If you defile it, I will defile you.' Now that is very serious. Therefore, we must take heed to our ways.

Another thing we saw, was that the Local Church was called, a House. Every time, 'House' is mentioned, in Scripture, it has got to do with the governmental dealings of God.

So when we read of the House we understand that government must be exercised to ensure this holiness. This is fundamental to the gatherings of God's people. I would that I, and all the rest of us, should understand, more clearly, just what this is all about.

Autonomy

Further in chapter 3, we looked at the Churches themselves, more carefully, and we found that in the Book of the Revelation, chapters 2 and 3, this local testimony is looked upon as a lamp-stand: Something which stands altogether, and abso-

Assembly Discipline

lutely, alone. There may be another lampstand down the town. There may even be another one up the town. Indeed, there may well be many others scattered throughout the land. But they stand altogether, and absolutely, on their own base. That means that one must not be controlled by any other. The one is not responsible to the other for its behaviour. It is responsible to no other Assembly under the sun. That is what you call, 'autonomous'. But it is responsible to God, and God alone, for its doctrines, for its Disciplines, for its outreaches and for everything else connected with it.

Therefore, the brethren that are in control of the meeting have a very serious position. They must make sure that they guide and see that the Assembly is taught the ways that be of God, otherwise they are failing in their task. Now these things are very, very serious.

There was an Assembly, in Belfast, 40 years ago, or more, where a problem arose and the overseeing brethren knew that they had not the capacity to stop it. They could do nothing with it. It was too deep seated, and it was not going to be long until the meeting was altogether divided. The government of the meeting decided that they would bring the best learned brother they could find, to minister from the Scripture on the subject in question. But he was not to give his advice. They got another brother, who was just as well read as the first and he was to sit and listen. Then the second brother was to answer to the first brother's remarks. Do you know what happened? It killed the trouble in a night. One night of teaching from the Holy Scriptures and that ended it. It was not advice, it was teaching.

Sometimes we feel that teaching is not necessary. Wait till the trouble comes! But then it will be too late. I am going to suggest to you that it is far, far better to give preventative medicine. Therefore, these things should be clearly taught amongst us so that we will know how to act when the time comes.

Now the strength of the Church lies in this very fact, that it has no ring or combine. It is not related to, nor is it subject to, nor is it answerable to, any other group.

Now, in a room we have a lamp. It shines altogether alone as if there was no another light in the room. It is utterly independent to any second light. It is 'autonomous'. That, of course,

Assembly Discipline

does not mean to say that the one light is sufficient. It would be lovely to have two, or three, or four lights shining in the room. So do not think that your Local Church is the only light needed on the face of this Earth. There are other areas where the light must shine also and, therefore, while we are not subject to the teaching of others, not subject to the government of others, not answerable to others, we are not independent of others. So that one light will shine in one vicinity, and another will shine in another vicinity, and while they are altogether and absolutely alone, yet they are dependent upon one another, not only for the spread of the Gospel but that each might be a pillar of the truth.

Overseers Responsibilities

In order to maintain holiness in this lovely place there must be Discipline, because we are not always walking a life reflective of this holiness. There are certain areas, as we shall see, in which we can go astray. Therefore, in order that holiness, and order, and truth, be maintained, there must be Discipline. If there is going to be Discipline, who is going to exercise it? Well, there are responsible, local brethren, called overseers, bishops, elders or pastors, among the Flock.

But, let me emphasise again, it is never called, 'their Flock'. The Scripture never speaks of an Assembly as being the Flock of the oversight. It is always, 'His Flock'. 'My Flock', says the Lord Jesus. These men, as under-shepherds, are responsible to the Chief Shepherd, as to how they lead, guide and instruct the people of God – His Flock. They are there on behalf of the Assembly, but are altogether answerable to God, as clearly taught in the Book of the Revelation, chapters 2 and 3. There, you will recall, it states in one place that the star is, (the government of one meeting) 'on His hand' – that is for display: So the government of the Church becomes an example to the Flock. But they are also said to be, 'in His hand', and that is control: So that the government of the fellowship is under the control of the Chief Shepherd. Oh, what serious, yet beautiful, things.

Why do so many clamour for overseership, when the office carries with it such serious, serious consequences? Indeed, according to the Epistle to the Hebrews, and I Peter, chapter 5, those dear overseeing brethren will have to stand before the Judgment Seat of Christ and give an account as to how they governed, taught, led and judged the Church of God.

Assembly Discipline

Order

God never intended the Assembly to be a place where every man does what is right in his own eyes. They did that in the Book of Judges and they ended up in havoc. Judges started off beautifully, with a man whose heart was full of love and it ended up with a man working as a woman at the mill. His name was Samson! One could look at the Book of Judges and see how well they did up to Gideon's day and then it began to fade, and before the book was over a man was doing woman's work. It is not right for a man to do what is right in his own eyes. He must subject himself to the government of the meeting.

I have been in the Assemblies of God's people a long time and, so, I speak from experience.

Once in my life I disobeyed my father. Just once! He did not hit me, he never said a word, but it broke my heart. Never again, till the day of my father's death, did I ever turn my tongue on him. Once was enough. I would love to be able to look back on life and say that I never disobeyed my father, but I cannot. I did it once.

Church Principles for Today

Once in my life, I turned my tongue on my mother and I thought, when I was at my work, that the day would never go in till I got home to make it up to her, to show her that I loved her from the very core of my being. You know, I would have got down and grovelled in the ashes, but I did not need to, did I? A mother's love is not that way. But I never forgot the sorrow of heart I experienced because I gave back cheek to my mother. I did it once, but that was enough.

What has that got to do with our subject? Once in my life I disobeyed the wishes of the government of the meeting. Once! It will not happen again with God's grace. It will not happen again. Now, I had done nothing to be ashamed of. I just disobeyed those who had the rule and did my own thing, and I did not get over it for years. Every man doing what was right in his own eyes. Brethren and sisters, it will not work. It is not God's order.

In the Assembly at Windsor, to which I belong, there is only one brother on the oversight older than I am. Just one. But I would not disobey that government. I feel happier when I have to submit to another. It is a sign of strength, and control, over yourself, rather than of weakness, when you do.

Assembly Discipline

Letters of Commendation

From the above then, oversight and Discipline are absolutely essential to the well-being of our meetings, as recorded in the Word of God. The very fact that there is such a thing as Discipline, shows that there must be Letters of Commendation, otherwise there is no reason for their use. What a beautiful thing to go through Scripture and to read of those nine Letters of Commendation, and find out what they are all about and the reasons for them. If there is no Discipline, there is no point in the Letter of Commendation – at least it takes away the strongest of its points.

The very fact that there must be Discipline in the meeting shows, to my simple mind, that there is a circle. It follows, therefore, that some are outside and some are inside, for everybody that is saved is not necessarily within the circle of the fellowship. (We will see that and prove that to you as the chapter continues.)

What if some person would come to the Assembly and the elders let him, in but then knew nothing of what he had taught somewhere else? The Lord alone can tell what havoc he could leave behind.

I remember going to Manchester for a year. When the year was over and I was coming back to my own Assembly, I said,

"Now, brethren, I need a Letter of Commendation".

They asked, "What do you need that for?"

I said that I was going home.

"But sure, that is your own Assembly you are going to."

I replied, "Indeed that is true, but they do not know, in Belfast, how I have behaved myself over here. They do not know whether I attended meetings or not. They do not know where I went on a Saturday afternoon. They do not know what I was doing on a Sunday. They do not know what I was teaching, or was listening to, when I was over here. Brethren, will you give me, please, a Letter of Commendation?"

I have it at home, it is precious to me. Signed, not only by the oversight but by every brother in the meeting.

When I came back home, to Belfast, I gave my Assembly the letter and so they knew that I had been behaving myself when I was across the water. It is a very dangerous thing to let a man come into the meeting of whom you know nothing. He could

Assembly Discipline

wreck the place, and then leave it, destroyed.

Delegation of God's Authority.

When we come to the delegation of government, or authority, we find that God alone is judge. Says the Person of the Lord Jesus Christ, in the Gospel according to John, 'The Father hath committed all judgment to Me' (John, chapter 5, verse 22). The Lord is the judge of all. That is why I have no right to judge you as to the way you live. This is what Romans is talking about: 'Don't you dare judge me, Sir, because I have one Master and He is in Heaven.' Neither should I judge you, for you have one Master and He is in Heaven! God never delegated judgment to anyone of us. Never!

But do you know what God has done? From the Epistle to the Romans, chapter 13, verse 1, He has taken of His government and has delegated it to the law of the land. So when the law of the land governs me for wrong doing, they are doing God's will. The Epistle to the Romans, chapter 13, verse 4, makes it perfectly plain that God has not given the sword to them in vain. I must stoop to the government of the land

Church Principles for Today

One day I was sitting in the car, along the side of the road, in Great Victoria Street, Belfast. There was a single yellow line on the side of the road. That means I could park there at certain times. There was also a notice hanging, and just to make sure I read it and it said that this is a no parking area between such and such a time. Well, I was outside the bounds of both the times, therefore, I was all right. A policeman came along. Good old fellow! He asked,

"Will you be long, you are holding up the traffic?"

I said, "I did not realise it, Sir. When I saw the single yellow line and read the notices, I thought I was all right."

He said, "You are not".

I said, "I will not be here any more than one second".

So, I started the car and away I went. Now, I went back and I looked at the line. There was just one. I looked at the notices, and I am perfectly satisfied that I was in the right. But if he told me the same tomorrow again, I would still move the car. We have to be subject to the laws of the land. God has delegated his governmental authority to them and they should use that sword. They are unrighteous to God if they do not.

Assembly Discipline

If we were to study, 'the Nations', we would find that God's sword will come down on them for not exercising that God-given authority.

God has delegated authority also to the government of the Assembly! He has taken of that authority which is His, and He has put it into the hands of the elders. They must exercise that governmental authority. If they do not, then because they are responsible to God, God will govern them. So, it is very serious.

Discipline

Now, there is one thing that I would like to mention here. It might seem out of context, but it is not. When you were saved, do you realise that God never touched your will? He never did, and He never shall! God shall never break your will. He has no reason in doing so. If God were to break your will, and break mine, we would be nothing but mechanical toys. Nothing else. But God does not want mechanical toys, He wants human beings. You have the power in your heart to say, "I will", or, "I will not", just as you wish. But if I know that I am doing wrong, yet I do it, remember, you are coming under government. God will not touch your will. You will die with a will of your own. I will tell you more: I see no Scripture to suggest that I will ever loose my will. God has not touched it and He never shall. Therefore, you can take this teaching to heart or you can say, "No". Just as you wish!

What is Discipline? It is sort of an instruction. It denotes, in Hebrews, chapter 12, the bringing up, and training, of children.

I have children, three of them, and I tried to train them. When they were young they did not know the way I thought and I knew that I understood far more than they, so I wanted them to think like me. I did not want to break their wills but I wanted them to think like me.

I taught them in different ways. I taught them by precept. "Look pets, 'Thou shalt not steal' (Exodus, chapter 20, verse 15). That is what God says. He does not like little children to steal. Sure you will not steal, pet? Never take that which is not your own. Look what it says, 'Do not lie'. Never tell a lie, pets, always tell the truth." Morning by morning, for about 15 to 20 minutes, until the wee family disintegrated by marriage, my wife and I sat and taught them the precepts of God. That was in-

Assembly Discipline

struction.

Then we did it another way. We did it by example. One day the child came in and he said something, and I said,

"Pet, where did you hear that?"

"I heard it in school, Daddy."

"Did you ever hear Mummy say that word?"

"No, I did not."

"Did you ever hear Daddy?"

"No, I did not."

"You will never go wrong if you only say the words that they say."

That is example.

Different ways to train a child and the idea was to instruct, and to train. But when my wee children did not do what they were told, and they knew very well they should have, there was another way – they were chastised. Oh, I am cruel, am I not?

I used to say to the child, "You know that is not right", and he would hang his head. "Go and get me a stick." Now, by the time he got a stick from the hedge outside, if I was angry, I was angry no longer, because it took him about an hour! Eventually he would come in with a little twig! So I would have to say, "You know what you have done wrong. Do you think that twig would be a proper chastisement for what you have done? Go and get me a stick." And away he would go again. Another half hour later he would come in with a bigger twig. "Now, that is still not big enough!" Away he would go again! And maybe, after an hour and a half, he would come in with a right size of a stick. Do you know there was no need for it then? He had already had the chastisement. So there would be a whole show of putting him over my knee, all sorts of displays, but at the end of it he got very little. But sometimes he had to get the stick.

When I look back on life I tell myself that I was too hard on my little children, far too hard. I can understand now how my father felt, when I was a young man, with my family around my knees. He did not like to see them being corrected. I could not understand it then, but I can understand it now. The father, generally gets little joy giving his child chastisement, but it brings forth fruit, nevertheless. This idea of Discipline, it is like the bringing up a child. It is to train.

Do you know that God has a stick? The Epistle to the He-

Assembly Discipline

brews, chapter 12, says that God has a stick and, now and again, He gives His children correction.

Let me say just one more thing to those of you who are parents. It says in Proverbs, chapter 22, verse 6, "Train up a child in the way he should go: and when he is old, he will not depart from it". That is not true! I have seen hundreds of children, well, a good number, depart. We had a dear old evangelist, in Northern Ireland, and we all loved him dearly. One day, while speaking at the Easter conference, in Belfast, he said, "Do you know the proper translation for that Scripture? It should read, 'Bring the child up in the way it should go and when he is old it will not depart from him'". I said, "Ah, that is it". So I went home and got my Bible, but that is not the way it said it in the Authorised Version. So I got hold of the Revised Version, but that is not the way it said it in the Revised either. I went over all the various translations I could get and it did not say it in any of them. So I scrapped it and kept an open mind.

I will tell you what it means now: Your little children are all absolutely different, and so you must train each child in the way, in the trend, of that child's mind and heart. You must see the way one little child is different from the other, and the way it, in turn, is different from the next and treat all of them in an entirely different way.

So also the government of the meeting. Is that not what Jude says, "And of some ... making a difference" (Jude, verse 22)? A word of rebuke to me, might run off me like water off a duck's back, but it might break another's heart! We are all different and we need to be handled differently.

I used to belong to Cregagh Street Gospel Hall, Belfast. I was very happy there. We had a dear old brother, who was a member, and he used to come into the Breaking of Bread meeting, on a Sunday, and sit at the back! What did the brethren do? Did they Discipline him? No, no! They all knew what had happened. He had had a row with his dear wife on the Saturday night! The oversight knew that and because his soul was sad, he sat at the back. They said, "It is all right, he will make it up before the night is over and he will be at the Lord's Table, next Sunday morning." And so he was! He would have been there for another three or four months and then one Sunday morning – sitting at the back again. More trouble! More rows! But they let him alone. They could have been hasty, you know. Wise brethren, who knew to handle each sheep differently.

Assembly Discipline

Types of Discipline

There are different types of Discipline in the Scripture. The first one is that God wants you to Discipline yourself. One way you can do that is by reading the Bible and putting it into practice, in your life. One of the reasons why God intended the saints to stay together was that we might learn ourselves. I did not say 'teach'. I am saying it properly: That we might 'learn ourselves'; that we might learn what we are.

If I were living in some island where there was no one but me, do you know that I would believe there was not another Christian like me on Earth? I would imagine, you see, that I was the best Christian ever, because I would have no one else to compare myself against. But when I come up against others and I have to live with them ... or when I come into the Assembly and find that the brethren do not see eye to eye with me ... then I go home and examine myself!

What God wants you to do, first of all, is to Discipline yourself. Now, if you do, there will never be any trouble. That is the end of it. But if you do not, do you know what will happen? Trouble will break out in the Assembly and when that happens the overseers will have to step in and will have to govern you, and discipline you. What if they fail to do this? Then God will intervene: He will discipline you and He will discipline the Assembly for having not disciplined you.

Can I teach that from Holy Scripture? Indeed, I could! Every word of it! We find in the Book of the Revelation, chapters 2 and 3, those that taught what they should not have been teaching and not a thing was done about it. Read what God says He will do at the end of those letters.

So we find these different ways in which Discipline is wrought. First of all, myself, then the Assembly and then the Lord. The Lord can discipline me and He can discipline the Assembly. We have already seen that God could discipline a meeting to such an extent that He could close the door altogether. He may let the devil affect the Church.

But let me make one thing abundantly clear: No Assembly may judge another. I have read the Bible from end to end, time, and time, and time, again. There are books in my Bible and I have studied every single verse in them and have written my own commentary on them. I have them at home. I am only say-

Assembly Discipline

ing that for one reason: I have never yet been able to find, in all my studies of the New Testament Scripture, where one Assembly was ever permitted to judge another. Never! If you do that, you are wrong. I can judge myself, the Assembly can judge me, the Lord can judge me, the Lord can judge the Assembly, but one Assembly must never judge another. That is not within the covers of this Bible.

Why Discipline?

Why this discipline? One of the reasons for Discipline is to keep evil from spreading.

My brother Sammy, and I, used to own a bakery. Now, my father was a baker to trade, so we gave him a job, every Friday night, in order to keep his old bones working; to keep him fit. I would go over for him, and bring him up to the bakery. Then, at five o'clock in the morning, he would ring me up and say, "I am standing here waiting for you". So, I would have to get up out of bed, and go to lift my father, leave him home, all of which took an hour and a half, or thereabouts.

Church Principles for Today

One night I said, "Look, father, I am not going to go home tonight. I am just going to sit here and watch you baking." It was an awful time! I could not keep my eyes open, what, with the heat and sleepiness and so on. Then he said, "If you would get up and do something, you would stay awake." So I stood beside him and he taught me how to make soda farls, and wheaten farls, and potato bread, and pancakes. Do you know that within about six months I was leaving him home at about one o'clock in the morning, instead of at five o'clock?

But I remember a lesson he gave me one night. He was making the dough and he said, "Son, weigh up the yeast, and weigh it accurately." I weighed up the yeast and put it in the breadmix. Then he said, "Weigh up the salt and weigh it accurately, for yeast hates salt and salt hates yeast, and they both work against one another." Then he said, "I want that dough to be absolutely ready at a certain time, that is why you must be exact with the yeast and the salt, for that yeast will permeate silently, and swiftly, and surely, until that great big dough is leavened throughout."

I was not thinking of the dough at all. I was thinking of the Local Assembly. One of the reasons why my God demands As-

Assembly Discipline

sembly Discipline is to prevent the evil from spreading, until the whole lump is leavened and the Assembly is destroyed, and their outreach, and their worship, and everything, is on the rocks. That could not happen! Could it not? Says I Corinthians, chapter 5, verse 6, " ... a little leaven leaveneth the whole lump."

I remember one day when I was advanced in baking! We were baking barm-bracks and we had put yeast into the mix. It became all puffed up. That is exactly what sin does. It puffs you up! The loaves, then, had to be coated and so my father said, "Now, what I want you to do, son, is to paint them." He had a special brush. It was camel's hair. So you beat up the egg and put the camel's hair brush into the beat-up egg and painted it on the bread. Father said, "Do it gently, because you cannot treat these puffed-up loaves whatever way you like. Do it very gently. If you do not do it right, you will knock them flat." So I put the brush in the mixture of egg. I went so carefully - but down the loaves went! He said, "What have you done? You have ruined them. Look. It is as easy as can be. This is the way you do it." So he took the brush, gave the bread a skite, and said, "That is the way you should do it".

Church Principles for Today

Oh, I could see the master's hand. When one of the brethren, or sisters, of the Assembly, is puffed up with sin, it is not everybody who can deal with it. You could knock them flat! It takes the master's hand, a man with ability, understanding and feeling to intervene.

Did you notice, while reading Philippians, chapter 4, that Paul refers to two girls who could not agree? He sent somebody to cure the trouble and do you know what he called the particular brother in question? He said, 'Thou true yoke-fellow, go help these two girls that cannot pull together.' Did you hear that. A 'true yoke-fellow', somebody who knew how to work with others. That is the one he sent to cure the trouble between those two sisters.

Sometime later, I said to my father, "Father, if you do not do something with these loaves, I declare, they are going to fill the bakery. They are getting bigger, and bigger ." He said, "I will soon stop them, son. Just you open that oven door and put them in." Do you know, as soon as the heat hit them, the leaven stopped? I said, "Father, they are not getting any bigger." He answered, "There are two things that leaven cannot stand. It cannot stand salt and it cannot stand a fire".

Assembly Discipline

Can you see it? Can you see why God speaks of leaven? It cannot stand the salt and it cannot stand the judgment.

Why should you exercise Discipline in the meeting? To stop the evil from spreading, for, "a little leaven leaveneth the whole lump".

It is to form character. Why do you think I chastised my little children? To show them how strong I was? To show them that I was the boss? No, no, no .... you do not do that with wee children! The reason why you train them, and discipline them, is to form character in them, so that they will be able to behave themselves when they grow up and when they go into other people's homes. I will say no more about that!

We discipline to preserve order in the House of God, to be a warning to others and to maintain the holy character of the Assembly.

Impartiality

Will you please notice, when we come to the New Testament, that when Discipline must be exercised, it must be in fairness. You have not to differentiate between the persons. It must have unanimity. If there is a doubt, do not judge. There must be no misplaced sympathy. Just as quickly, I would judge my own child, as I would yours. You know, as well as I, that there are people you like and others that you do not like. I do not know why. Maybe it is the shape of their nose! I cannot tell you. But when it comes to Discipline, this is the work of God. There must be no partiality and it must never be done on the grounds of suspicion. The Lord demanded that in the Old Testament, and in the New. You must be sure of your ground because the result could, otherwise, be very serious, as I will show you.

Forms of Assembly Discipline

Now when we come to the act of Discipline itself, we find that there are two major forms, in the New Testament. There can be the kind of Discipline where the person is put out of the fellowship altogether.

(Now, if there is no inside and no outside, how could you put him out? If there is no inside and no outside, he could come back next week. We read, in the Bible that some, 'came in';

Assembly Discipline

that some were, 'brought in'; that some, 'went out', and that some were 'put out'. If there is no circle of fellowship, these Scriptures have no meaning. There must be a, 'putting out' and a, 'going out', a 'coming in' and a 'bringing in', otherwise Assembly Discipline has no meaning. This is very, very serious and very sad.)

Some think that this man, in I Corinthians, chapter 5, was put out and in II Corinthians, chapters 2 and 7, he was brought in again. I do not think so. I remember years ago having a lovely discourse with the late Mr. William Lavery on this point. He said,

"Rowan, you are destroying the book by saying that these two men were different individuals."

I said, "I am not, Mr Lavery. You show me, in II Corinthians, chapter 2, that the man that is being spoken of, is the man in I Corinthians, chapter 5."

No one has ever been able to satisfactorily answer me. Indeed, the more I study II Corinthians, chapters 2 and 7, the more determined I am, in my own soul, that the man, in question, is not the man, of I Corinthians, chapter 5. The man in I Corinthians, chapter 5, was put outside the Assembly for the destruction of his very flesh. So this 'putting out' is a very serious thing.

Brethren and sisters, you have to watch yourselves. When you are 'inside' the fellowship there is that atmosphere to keep you close to Him; there is that atmosphere of control. But once you go 'outside' the meeting, you are beyond all guidance.

Now, I have not said, for one moment, that a man who is put out cannot be brought in. I did not say that. What I did say was that this man, in II Corinthians, chapter 2, is not the man, in I Corinthians, chapter 5. The man who erred, in I Corinthians, was put out for the destruction of his flesh and yet his spirit was saved. Amazing thought!

The form of error, whereby you can be excommunicated, is moral lapse: Fornication, covetousness, idolatry, reviling, drunkenness and extortion. They are all in I Corinthians, chapter 5.

Before an oversight exercises Discipline in that form it must be very, very careful to know all the facts. The reason for this is because once the brother is put out of the meeting, or once the

Assembly Discipline

sister is put out, those individuals are put in the lap of the devil himself. That is a most awful, and fearful, state of affairs and so the oversight has to be careful. But if the brother, or sister, does err in any of these ways then there must be chastisement, there must be rejection from the Assembly fellowship and more than that, "with such an one no not to eat" (I Corinthians, chapter 5, verse 11). So, while they must be put out, the oversight must take things gently and study the case, very carefully, as to just what has taken place and then, if applicable, they must be put out.

But there is another reason for which a man can be put out. It is very seldom that I have seen it in operation, indeed, I have seen it just once. If a man is an unsound teacher then he must be put out! Titus, chapter 3, tells us of that. The propagation of unsound doctrine. I tell you, it would take a well read oversight to discover that.

What about doctrines concerning the sonship of the Lord Jesus? What about doctrines concerning His deity and humanity, or concerning His atonement?

Not so very long ago I was in a meeting and one of my beloved brethren said something about the Person of our Lord Jesus Christ, which cast a shadow on His humanity. I would not have said that he should be put out, I would not give advice, but I certainly think that he should have been approached, at least. You must never cast a shadow on the deity of Christ, nor a shadow on His humanity, for if you take away from one, or the other, the result is that we have no Saviour!

If you were to look at Titus, chapter 3, verses 9 - 14, you would see for yourself that propagation of unsound doctrine should result in rejection. If you do not, it will wreck the meeting.

We saw, in an earlier chapter, that if you were to read the history of the Assemblies, you would find that those which are closed have been destroyed in one of two ways. They have been destroyed by brethren, or sisters, who fell morally or they have been destroyed by brethren, or sisters, who fell doctrinally. Tell me, which of the two is the worse? Moral? No - doctrinal! The moral error can touch any member of the meeting but the doctrinal error will only touch the teachers. Once they have been swayed by doctrinal error, the meeting is destroyed. A very, very serious thing.

Assembly Discipline

But there is a third reason. For years, and years, I looked at Matthew's Gospel, chapter 18, and could never understand it. I listened, for years and years, to the teachings of my beloved brethren and still never understood it! So I got in touch with one of the greatest teachers I knew, at a conference in England, and asked him about my problem and so we sat down and talked about it. I think, that by the time our little talk was over, I had the idea behind Matthew, chapter 18 – and it is also very serious.

It could be a very small thing between you and me, a very small thing indeed, but it is dividing us, nevertheless. So, because I have wronged you in some personal way, you come and see me about it, but you might as well talk to the wall as talk to me. So the problem still exists. According to Matthew chapter 18, you come again, but this time you take one, or two, brethren with you, but you might as well talk to the wall as talk to me. So the problem still exists. It is a very personal problem, but it is there. So you come again, but now you take the overseers of the Church to me, but you might as well talk to the wall as talk to me. Now here is the point: The government of the meeting has got to make a decision and that decision is binding. Whatever they say I must be subject to it or it may be my expulsion from the meeting.

This shows to me how exceedingly important it is to recognise the government in the Assembly. There may be men there that I do not think should be there but that is not my affair. It may be that you think you should be there and you are not there, but you leave that with God. The thing that is incumbent upon us all is to be in subjection to the decisions of the government of the meeting, unless they ask us to do something which is morally, or doctrinally, wrong.

So, there are three reasons why one can be expelled: moral error, doctrinal error, or a little matter that snowballed to such an extent that the government of the meeting must make a decision, which is final and altogether binding upon the whole Assembly. See Figure 7.1:

Moral Error:	Fornication	
	Covetousness	
	Idolatory	
	Railing	
	Drunkenness	
	Extortion	I Corinthians, 5
Doctrinal Error:	Unsound Doctrine	Titus, 3
Personality Clashes		Matthew, 18

Figure 7.1: **Reasons for Excommunication**

Assembly Discipline

But then there are other matters for Discipline, but for which excommunication is not required. For instance, we find in Titus, chapter 1, verses 9 - 14, an unprofitable talker in the Assembly. He is not teaching division. No, he is not like the man in Titus, chapter 3. He is not wrecking the meeting because of being doctrinally off line. He is just an unprofitable talker. We might call him a sort of a blatherer, at least, he is wasting the time of the saints. Now what are you going to do with him? You cannot put him out, he is not in that category at all. But you cannot continue to let him waste the saints' time in unprofitable talk and ministry. (Mind you, brethren, could it be that if we studied the Corinthian passage that we would find that while we do not agree with one man ministry, I Corinthians does not agree with any man ministry? Would that we could learn that. Sometimes I feel that the pendulum has swung from one extreme to the other. For while it is not given for one man to be the 'be-all' and 'end-all', it is not given for all men to minister to the saints.) What are you going to do with this soul? It tells you what you have got to do - rebuke him, and rebuke him sharply. It does not say that this is to be done in a public way. Read Titus, chapter 1, carefully, and it will show you exactly what has to be done to that dear brother.

Church Principles for Today

Remember, I mentioned earlier that sometimes you must deal with brethren in different ways because we are not all built the same? Just as little children are different, so are the dear Christians. I can see perfectly clearly, why God desires that the governors of the Local Church are those that have brought up children: Because as the children are all different - so are the saints, and so differences have got to be made in dealing with them.

Then, in Romans, chapter 16, you get another kind of a man. A man who is a division maker. He is not trying to actually divide the meeting into parts but he is causing problems by one thing and another. He is not a sect maker but he is causing divisions in the meeting. He is propagating his own little pet views of things and every time he gets up to say a word, or two, you can rest assured that you know what he will be speaking about. Some wee thing has caught his heart, and mind, and he cannot get away from it. But because of this, he is causing divisions in the meeting. Some are for him; some are against him. What are you going to do? It says that you will have to reprove him. You will have to mark and eventually avoid him, if necessary, but he must be dealt with. See Figure 7.2:

Assembly Discipline

Unprofitable Ministry - Titus, 1 - Rebuke
Devision Makers - Romans, 16 - Reproof

Figure 7.2: Non-excomunication Methods of Correction

Sometimes the overseers themselves, wonderful as they may be, can err. When they err, it is an exceedingly serious thing because they are the government of the Church. It is they who are to exercise Discipline on God's behalf and on behalf of the meeting, so they themselves must be very much above reproof. But sometimes they can err. What is going to happen now? They may have to be put out of the meeting, certainly. They may be doctrinally wrong, they may be morally wrong. But there are other ways that they can sin and when that happens it is perfectly plain, from I Timothy, chapter 5, that they must be rebuked - and in public - and will you notice, they are the only persons to be rebuked in public. This is because of the highly esteemed, and public, position that they hold. See Figure 7.3:

Overseers
- Moral Error   - ⎫
- Doctrinal Error   - ⎬ Excommunication
- Personality Clashes   - ⎭
- Unprofitable Ministry - ⎫ Public Rebuke
- Division Makers   - ⎭

Figure 7. 3:   Correcting Overseers

Church Principles for Today

Now, I think I have written enough to have sufficiently shown you how essential it is that there must be Discipline in the meeting, in order that the standard of the holiness of God might be built up.

So Discipline is absolutely essential in Church life. I have sought to point out, very particularly, at the beginning of the chapter, the reason for all these things, rather than the actual disciplinary measures themselves. I sought to show the necessity of Discipline. Then, I pointed out some of the reasons why God demands Discipline in the meeting:

1) To keep evil from spreading.

2) To keep or to form character.

3) To preserve order.

4) To be a warning to others.

5) To maintain Holiness.

May the Lord help us to Disipline ourselves.

Chapter 8

Headship

As an introduction to the subject of Headship, I want to quote three passages of Scripture. The first in:

I Corinthians, chapter 11, verses 2 - 16:

"Now I praise you, brethren, that ye remember me in all things, and keep the ordinances, as I delivered them to you. But I would have you know, that the head of every man is Christ; and the head of the woman is the man; and the head of Christ is God. Every man praying or prophesying, having his head covered, dishonoureth his head. But every woman that prayeth or prophesieth with her head uncovered dishonoureth her head: for that is even all one as if she were shaven. For if the woman be not covered, let her also be shorn: but if it be a shame for a woman to be shorn or shaven, let her be covered. For a man indeed ought not to cover his head, forasmuch as he is the image and glory of God: but the woman is the glory of the man. For the man is not of the woman; but the woman of the man. Neither was the man created for the woman; but the woman for the man. For this cause ought the woman to have power on her head because of the angels. Nevertheless neither is the man without the woman, neither the woman without the man, in the Lord. For as the woman is of the man, even so is the man also by the woman; but all things of God. Judge in yourselves: is it comely that a woman pray unto God uncovered? Doth not even nature itself teach you, that, if a man have long hair, it is a shame unto him? But if a woman have long hair, it is a glory to her: for her hair is given her for a covering. But if any man seem to be contentious, we have no such custom, neither the churches of God."

Then, in I Corinthians, chapter 14, verses 33 - 35:

"For God is not the author of confusion, but of peace, as in

Headship

all churches of the saints. Let your women keep silence in the churches: for it is not permitted unto them to speak; but they are commanded to be under obedience, as also saith the law. And if they will learn any thing, let them ask their husbands at home: for it is a shame for women to speak in the church."

And finally, in I Epistle to Timothy, chapter 2, verses 8 - 15:

"I will therefore that men pray every where, lifting up holy hands, without wrath and doubting. In like manner also, that women adorn themselves in modest apparel, with shamefacedness and sobriety; not with braided hair, or gold, or pearls, or costly array. But (which becometh women professing godliness) with good works. Let the woman learn in silence with all subjection. But I suffer not a woman to teach, nor to usurp authority over the man, but to be in silence. For Adam was first formed, then Eve. And Adam was not deceived, but the woman being deceived was in the transgression. Notwithstanding she shall be saved in childbearing, if they continue in faith and charity and holiness with sobriety."

Church Principles for Today

Introduction

The subjects we are dealing with are delicate, and one has to be very careful about the way they are delivered, lest we should offend. Therefore, I trust, with the help of the Lord, that I am delivering them gently, but also faithfully, so that we will not stray from the truth that is plainly taught in the Word of God. The last thing that we want to do is to hurt a soul.

We come now to an exceedingly delicate question, the beloved womenfolk - the sisters in the fellowship. I would not say anything to hurt you. You know that! All I am going to do is state plainly, if I can, what is clearly taught in I Corinthians, chapter 11; in I Corinthians, chapter 14; and in I Timothy, chapter 2.

Headship

Now there are some things on the very surface and to which we will all readily agree. I know we will. One of the first things that you will understand perfectly plainly, is that God is the Head of Christ. You will all agree with that, because it says so. It says also, that Christ is the Head of the man, and we would all agree with that. Then it says that the man is the Head of the

Headship

woman. That is what it says. So, God is the Head of Christ; Christ is the Head of the man; the man is the Head of the woman.

We would find, if we went back to the Book of Genesis, that the woman was created second. Man was formed first of all and then the woman. That did not put her in Subjection to the man, will you notice? It has nothing to do with Subjection, but it did make him the Head. See Figure 8:1.

God is the Head of Christ

Christ is the Head of Man

Man is the Head of Woman

Figure 8.1: **Headship**

Then, what happened in Genesis, chapter 3? The woman made a mistake. She transgressed. She was the first in transgression and because of that she became subject to her husband. Now, that is different to Headship!

So, in creation, man was first and that made him the Head, but in transgression the woman was first and that put her in

Subjection. So we find these two things relevant to the beloved sisters. Can you see them?

This idea of Headship is dealt with, in I Corinthians, chapter 11; the idea of Subjection is dealt with, in I Corinthians, chapter 14; and the two of them are dealt with, in I Timothy, chapter 3. See Figure 8:2.

First in Creation, therefore, Man is Head	- I Corinthians, 11.
First in Transgression, therefore, Woman is in Subjection	- I Corinthians, 14.
Headship and Subjection	- I Timothy, 3.

Figure 8.2: **Headship and Subjection**

When we look at Headship, we must ask how this doctrine is to be symbolised. God wants us all to appreciate and recognise it and, therefore, it must be symbolised.

Let me give you an example. We would read that we have died with Christ and are buried with Christ. Good! How is it symbolised? By Baptism! So also does God want Headship and Subjection to be symbolised and He wants us to bear those symbols. A young woman will wear the symbol of a ring to

Headship

show that she is married, so also God wants us to wear the symbols of Headship and of Subjection.

How can I show the symbol of a person being my Head? How can I show the symbol of a person being in Subjection? It is very easy. God has done it very, very clearly. He uses our natural head to be the symbol of Headship but he uses the tongue as the symbol of Subjection.

Now, we have already agreed that Christ is the Head of the man. Notice what happens. Man is going to show that Christ is his Head, he is going to symbolise that Christ is his Head - by his physical head, because that is the symbol of Headship. So also a woman is going to show that man is her Head, by her physical head. Because God has made it that our head is the symbol of Headship.

Now, when we appreciate that, things begin to become clear. The woman is going to show the Headship of the man, by her head, but she is going to show her Subjection by her tongue. Now once those things are clearly seen, things begin to fall perfectly, and clearly, into place. See Figure 8:3.

| Symbol of Headship | - | our natural head |
| Symbol of Subjection | - | our tongue |

Figure 8.3: The Corresponding Symbols

However, if I am going to show that Christ is my Head, and my wife is going to show that I am her Head, we must then display the symbol in a different way. Your head, beloved brother, has got to display the Headship of Christ and your head, dear sister, has got to display the Headship of man, but the two displays must have a difference, for Christ is altogether different from the man.

When God made man, He made him with His hands, out of the red clay. So when I look at a man I see the glory, and the image, of the invisible God. The man reflects God in all His glory. But the woman, she was made out of the man, so she reflects the man's glory. The man was created but the woman was builded, (I say that rather than built). Therefore, in this man I must see displayed the beautiful glory of God but in that woman I must see the glory of the man. Tell me, am I right

Headship

when I say that these glories are different? I am, of course. Surely when a man displays the glory of God, that display would be altogether different from the display of a man's glory.

Further, I understand that in the presence of God, the glory of the man must be hidden, whereas the glory of God must be displayed.

How does a man show that Christ is his Head? By his head. But we all have heads, both women and men, therefore, I, as a man, will have to do something with my head to display the glory of God and the Headship of Christ. What has God decreed to be the symbol? Brethren, short hair! So the man displays the glory of God, and displays the Headship of Christ, by the way he wears the hair on his head. Because the glory of God must be absolutely manifested, then I can see perfectly clearly that the man's natural head should be seen, and it is seen by his having his hair short.

I do not mean for one moment that he has got to have it shaven. It will come that way soon enough. It does not say how short it should be, but we will see how short it should be by the end of the chapter. So the man shows the glory of God exposed, and the fact that Christ is his Head, by having short hair.

Oh, but we said that the glory of God is different than the glory of man. So what the woman is going to do, is to show that man is her Head, and she is his glory, by her head. But in the presence of God, man's glory is not to be seen, thus, the woman will have long hair, so that her head is all covered up, typifying that her husband's glory is out of sight. See Figure 8:4.

Man	-	shows the Headship of Christ	- short hair.
Man	-	shows the Glory of Christ	- short hair.
Woman	-	hides the Headship of Man	- long hair.
Woman	-	hides the Glory of Man	- long hair.

Figure 8.4: **The Hair Question**

It is a nice thing, when the brethren who minister on the Lord's Day morning, look around the meeting and see the beloved sisters with their hair long, and when they see that, do you know what should immediately jump into their minds? I am out of sight! But equally, when the beloved brother gets up to minister, and sees all the brethren with their short hair, he should also remember that the glory of God is not out of sight and so he guides his ministry to

Headship

hide himself but to glorify the Person of God, and of Christ.

Now, it is one thing to do what we are told, but how should we show that we agree with God? How does the man show, for example, that he agrees that his glory? - Christ, must alone be seen. He does not wear a covering on his head. In doing so, he not only does what God tells him to do, but agrees with what God tells him to do.

As such, then his Head, Christ, is very, very well exposed! So God demands that his hair is short, and the man's 'Amen' to that is that he will not wear a hat.

Now the woman is different. She wears the long hair because God said so, so that the glory of her husband is out of sight. But she shows that she agrees with God, when she puts a covering on top of her hair. So that her Head, the man, is doubly out of sight!

Therefore, it is not a matter of custom for ladies to wear coverings, and men not to; it is not a matter of tradition; it is not a matter of fashion; it is a matter of doctrine. See Figure 8:5.

Man	-	wears no covering on his head
Woman	-	wears a covering on her head.

Figure 8.5: Our Agreement Regarding God's Order of Headship

But there is another interesting comment, in our passage. It tells us, perfectly plainly, that the angels are looking on and learning. It says this in I Corinthians, chapter 11. There is no doubt that the angels are looking on, but what are they looking at? It would almost seem to me that they are not looking at the men but rather at the women. That would seem to be the context of the passage, read it carefully and see if I am right.

Now there are two ways of looking at this particular passage. I will give you them both and you can study them both at your leisure and decide which of the two you prefer. What do these angels see? They see her long hair and they see her, 'Amen', by the putting on of her covering. What do they learn? They learn that man is out of sight and they learn that the glory of God has to be revealed. What all else the angels learn, I do not know, but whatever God is teaching through the women, He can only show them, what He wants to show them, when she displays her covered head.

Headship

But there is another argument. Away back in the Book of Genesis, chapter 6, something terrible happened: Angels came down and married women. There is no question at all in my mind, indeed, I am absolutely persuaded, in my heart, that the sons of God, in Genesis, chapter 6, were angelic beings and that they came down and married women. Now, that did not please God. It is no wonder He sent the flood. It is no wonder, indeed. That happened once. God does not want it to happen again. Has God told the angels, 'When you look at women, you will remember that they are not for you, but for men! Look at the hair'? Is that what God has in mind? If this is so, then when the angels look at the hair of the woman they remember God saying, that she is man's glory, therefore, 'She is not for you, she was made for the man'.

It could almost seem, from the way we are talking, that the gentleman is superior to the woman and the poor woman is only a chattel. The passage is very careful, very, very careful. When God speaks about Headship, He never speaks about inferiority. Never! The man is not looked upon as superior to the woman, even though he is her Head. Neither is the woman looked upon as inferior to the man even though she is in Subjection. They are looked upon as absolutely essential to one another, in the Lord. So the man says to his beloved wife, "You know, before you came I was here. How long I was here it does not matter, but I was here before you came. And furthermore, if I had not been here you would have never been here." So the man sticks out his chest in pride: How superior he is! Then the woman says, very gently, to him, "That is true, my dear, but if there had not been a me, there would not have been any more of you." So that puts him in his place! The passage is very, very clear, therefore, when it says, " ... the man is not without the woman and the woman is not without the man in the Lord" (I Corinthians, chapter 11, verse 11). So, it is not a matter of inferiority. They are both essential.

There is nothing more beautiful than to see the man and the woman working together for the Lord, each in their proper sphere.

God is the Head of Christ. Is Christ inferior to God? God is the Head of Christ. Is God superior to Christ? You only have to read the like of Philippians, chapter 2, and masses of other passages, to see perfectly clearly that Christ is never inferior to God and, further, that God is never looked upon as superior to Christ. God is the Head of Christ but there is no question of inferiority.

Headship

Does the passage go a little further? It does. You beloved sisters, I am going to say it very gently, you would not like to go bald, would you? Men do not worry about things like that. It will not be long, if I keep on the way I am going, until I am bald. Do you know, it does not worry me one single bit? But it would certainly worry a woman! It would nearly make her mentally unbalanced to know that she is losing all her hair. Why is this? Is there something in a woman's nature that rebels against her having no hair?

During the war years, if the Nazi's wanted to bring a woman to the lowest shame, do you know what they did? They just shaved her head and made her walk up and down the streets of Paris with her head shaven. Do you know why? Because that poor woman could feel no greater shame than to have her head shaven. Men do not worry about that. Why? Nature does not object to a man having a bald head but it does object, very strongly, to a woman. You see, her hair is given to her, naturally, for a covering. She loves it, she really honestly does, and by chance she cuts it now and again, nevertheless, she would never like to be bald. Nature rebels against it.

Inconsistencies

Then, Paul the Apostle goes on to speak, in I Corinthians chapter, 14, of the tongue; how that a woman is going to show her Subjection by her tongue. By her head she is going show Headship. By her tongue she is going to show Subjection. Two entirely different things. By her very silence in the gathering of the Church, she displays her Subjection. By her covered head, that is, with long hair, she displays the man's Headship and by the fact that she covers her hair, shows that she is agreeing with what God has said, that man's glory should be out of sight in His presence, but by her keeping silent she displays her Subjection.

Let us look at just one, or two, inconsistencies that might happen. For instance, here is a woman, she has a hat on and she is praying in public to God. She is right in one way but she is wrong in the other. Look at the foolishness of it; the inconsistency of it. She has a hat on. "Yes indeed, man is my Head but I am not in Subjection." An inconsistency!

What would happen, if a woman were silent in the meeting, thus, acknowledging her Subjection to the man, but she had her

Headship

hair short. What is she doing now? It is the other way about? By the very fact that she is silent she shows that she is in Subjection. But her head is uncovered and by that she shows that he is not her Head.

It is wrong if one of them is wrong. It is only right if both are right. Her head covered, she acknowledges the man is her Head; her tongue is silent, she acknowledges she is in Subjection.

Then, of course, you could disagree with God. Scripture takes care of that also. It takes care of it in verse 16, of I Corinthians, chapter 11, 'and some will be contentious.' What about a woman who is silent in the meeting? She is agreeing that she is subject to the man. She has long hair, lovely soul, so she agrees that man is her Head. But she has no hat on. Now what is wrong. She is saying, "God says that man is my Head, that is why I have long hair. God says I am Subjection to the man that is why I do not speak, but I do not agree with God, that is why I have no hat on!"

Then one day she understands that man is her Head, God says it and so she has long hair. Then she says that she is in Subjection to the man, so she does not speak. Then she says that this is what God says and that she agrees with every word that God says. So on goes a hat. So the hat is her, 'Amen', to what God has plainly taught. (That is what you did in your Baptism. You just said, 'Amen'.) See Figure 8:6.

The Woman is silent	- she is in subjection to man due to being first in transgression.
The woman has long hair	- man is her head, due to him being created first.
The woman has a head covering	- she shows that she is in complete agreement with God.

Figure 8.6: The Woman's Stance

Beloved sisters, what happens when you are at home at night and you kneel down at the bedside, do you cover your head? I have heard the brethren argue about this for years. They have said this has got absolutely nothing to do with the home life of the beloved sister. All right then, brother, before you get down tonight to pray, will you put your hat on and then bow your knees before God and seek his face? Do you know what I believe? I believe that there is not a brother who would have the audacity to get down on his two knees before God and put his hat on. Not one! Why? I almost believe that we would be afraid. You would say, "I dare not do that, that would be dis-

Headship

honouring God." Well, the same applies to the beloved sister!

It used to be, that ladies covered their heads in the home but that is nearly done away with now. I remember years ago, at a local conference, when this very passage, of I Corinthians, chapter 11, was under discussion and that dear man, Mr Campbell, spoke so gently. He said, "My brethren, I have visited the beloved saints for years, and have prayed in all their homes, but never once has a sister covered her head. Was I wrong? Should I not have prayed then?" One of the teaching brethren, that was there, said a beautiful thing. He said, "Beloved brother, this thou shoulds't have done and not to have left the other undone."

I will leave it to your own judgment, whether it is right, or wrong, in the home. I am absolutely satisfied, in my heart, that it is right.

Then, of course, there are little inconsistencies on the man's side, if he has long hair. What is he doing? The man with the long hair says,

"Christ is not my Head."

But, did we not agree, from Genesis, chapter 3, that you are the glory of God.

"Oh yes", the long haired man says, "But I do not want anybody to see God's glory."

Is there a Christian that would say that? Remember, your head is the symbol of Headship and, therefore, you should want to show your Head as much as it is conveniently possible. These are the inconsistencies that take place. See Figure 8:7.

| The Man has short hair | - | Christ is his Head and He must be seen. |
| Man has no covering | - | he agrees that Christ is his Head. |

Figure 8.7: **The Man's Stance**

All this is not a matter of custom. It is not a matter of fashion. It is a matter of doctrine.

Now, beloved sister, just how long do you think your hair should be? You, brother, how short should yours be? Should you, Christian lady, ever cut it at all? Should you, Christian sir, cut it until you shave it? For if the woman's hair must never be touched, then if we are consistent, then the best way to display your Head, my brother, is to shave all your hair off!

Headship

Let me ask you a question. You ask it yourself, you beloved sisters, you beloved brethren. Have you understood the doctrine? Do you now appreciate that the man is the glory of God and that glory must be displayed. How does he do it? By his head! Is your hair short enough to display that truth? Are you satisfied? Can I go down on my knees tonight and say, "Father, my head displays Thy glory"? Is your conscience clear? If so, I am going to suggest to you, that you are all right.

Beloved sister, you know the doctrine. You are the glory of the man, but remember, that glory which must be hidden. You are going to display the truth, that man came first, then you. He is your Head. Tell me beloved sister, is your hair long enough to display that truth? Are you happy? Is your conscience clear? Would you kneel down before God tonight and say, "Father, I see Thy truth so clearly, and I believe that my hair is long enough to display the teaching that man's glory must be hidden in Thy presence"? Can you say that? If you can, I am going to suggest to you, that you are all right.

The Woman's Place

Then there is another point we must clarify. It is said that the poor woman is not allowed to teach, but Scripture does not say that! It says that in the Church she is not allowed to teach. Do not say that the Scripture never allows a woman to teach. That is not so. Could I turn you to a passage where it says that the woman could teach? Of course I could. All I have got to do is turn to Titus, chapter 2, and it says, 'You older women, take these younger women aside and teach them'. They can do that. Who, on earth, would be better to teach a young woman, than an older one?

Do you think the brethren could teach the young sisters? I should think not. Sometimes, it happens that young sisters have problems that they would not want to tell mummy. Would it not be beautiful if there was an older sister, in the Assembly, to whom they could go, and tell their troubles and get instruction? I tell you, there is a work for older sisters to be done in teaching – teaching young sisters: How they should behave themselves at home with their husbands; in the Church with the saints; and in the world. Who better to teach a woman, than a woman?

I read, somewhere, that 60% of all the missionaries on the field are women. Imagine. Who can do their work better?

Headship

I remember well, at an Easter conference, some years ago, when one of the beloved brethren said something very harsh about the beloved sisters. One of the missionary brethren listened carefully, then said a very gentle, and kindly, word. He said, "I am a missionary, in Angola. You take the sisters out of Angola and I will have to come home." Oh, there is a place for the dear sisters.

Who can bring up the children like a woman? Who gives her heart like a woman?

Who stands behind the man, but the woman? If you were to look at the Book of Judges, you would find that the very first man, Othniel, was a success as a result of a woman. The very last judge, Samson, was brought down to be like a woman - as a result of a woman. The woman behind a man is the be-all and end-all of that man. Like Othniel, she can make him, or like Samson, she can break him.

I could consider Miriam and her song, Phebe and her faithfulness, Dorcas and her good works. I could go over to Priscilla and Aquilla, who laid down their neck (not necks), working together as one, not inferior, not superior, but each in his and her sphere working together for God.

Sister, let no one take your crown.

Chapter 9

THE GRACE OF GIVING

In this book we have been dealing with Church Truths, and I trust I have not made them too difficult. Sometimes, we practise these Truths, but we do not know why. As a result of this, we sometimes see what we practice to be solely tradition and, therefore, we may feel that we want to reject them and not to practise them at all. Then again, sometimes, because we are not taught these beautiful Truths, we can be led astray by some 'wind of doctrine'.

I have sought to prove to you the doctrine behind many of the practices of our Church gatherings and in light of that soon coming Judgement Seat of Christ, when we will have to give an account, as to our obedience to these things, then it would behove us to put them into practice.

Now this is the last chapter and we are going to read a portion from the Old Testament and then one from the New.

Our first reading is from:
Leviticus, chapter 23, verses 9 - 14:

"And the LORD spake unto Moses, saying, Speak unto the children of Israel, and say unto them, When ye be come into the land which I give unto you, and shall reap the harvest thereof, then ye shall bring a sheaf of the firstfruits of your harvest unto the priest: And he shall wave the sheaf before the LORD, to be accepted for you: on the morrow after the sabbath ..."

Now if the Sabbath was a Saturday, then it is evident that the "morrow after the sabbath" was a Sunday.

"... the priest shall wave it. And ye shall offer that day when ye wave the sheaf an he lamb without blemish of the first year for a burnt offering unto the LORD. And the meat offering thereof shall be two tenth deals of fine flour mingled with oil, an offering made by fire unto the LORD for a sweet savour:

THE GRACE OF GIVING

and the drink offering thereof shall be of wine, the fourth part of an hin. And ye shall eat neither bread, nor parched corn, nor green ears, until the selfsame day that ye have brought an offering unto your God: it shall be a statute for ever throughout your generations in all your dwellings."

Then, in the **Epistle of Paul to II Corinthians, chapter 8, verses 1 - 24:**

"Moreover, brethren, we do you to wit of the grace of God bestowed on the churches of Macedonia; How that in a great trial of affliction the abundance of their joy and their deep poverty abounded unto the riches of their liberality. For to their power, I bear record, yea, and beyond their power they were willing of themselves; Praying us with much intreaty that we would receive the gift, and take upon us the fellowship of the ministering to the saints. And this they did, not as we hoped, but first gave their own selves to the Lord, and unto us by the will of God. Insomuch that we desired Titus, that as he had begun, so he would also finish in you the same grace also. Therefore, as ye abound in everything, in faith, and utterance, and knowledge, and in all diligence, and in your love to us, see that ye abound in this grace also. I speak not by commandment, but by occasion of the forwardness of others, and to prove the sincerity of your love. For ye know the grace of our Lord Jesus Christ, that, though he was rich, yet for your sakes he became poor, that ye through his poverty might be rich. And herein I give my advice: for this is expedient for you, who have begun before, not only to do, but also to be forward a year ago, Now therefore perform the doing of it; that as there was a readiness to will, so there may be a performance also out of that which ye have. For if there be first a willing mind, it is accepted according to that man hath, and not according to that he hath not. For I mean not that other men be eased, and ye burdened: But by an equality, that now at this time your abundance may be a supply for their want, that their abundance also may be a supply for your want: that there may be equality: As it is written, He that had gathered much had nothing over; and he that had gathered little had no lack. But thanks be to God, which put the same earnest care into the heart of Titus for you. For indeed he accepted the exhortation; but being more forward, of his own accord he went unto you. And we have sent with him the brother, whose praise is in the gospel throughout all the churches; And not that only, but who was also chosen of the churches to travel with us with this grace, which is administered by us to the glory of the same Lord, and declaration of your ready mind: Avoiding this,

THE GRACE OF GIVING

that no man should blame us in this abundance which is administered by us: Providing for honest things, not only in the sight of the Lord, but also in the sight of men. And we have sent with them our brother, whom we have oftentimes proved diligent in many things, but now much more diligent, upon the great confidence which I have in you. Whether any do inquire of Titus, he is my partner and fellow helper concerning you: or our brethren be inquired of, they are the messengers of the churches, and the glory of Christ. Wherefore shew ye to them, and before the churches, the proof of your love, and of our boasting on your behalf."

Introduction

As already stated, the purpose of this book has been to deal with some of the Truths connected with public gatherings, as set out by Holy Scripture.

We have seen that the Church had its inception by the coming of the Holy Spirit and the Baptism into the Spirit, of the first saints, in Acts, chapter 2. That happened on the first day of the week. It happened on the day after the Sabbath.

Then we saw, as we progressed, that God had no schisms in that great Body and it was His desire that the members should gather together in what we call, 'Assembly Fellowship'. This was necessary for a number of reasons, but one of them was that the saints should be helped in their day-to-day salvation. This was because a person could never become holy when he was alone but, rather, it was when he was in the company of others that he began to see himself as others saw him; he began to see what was wrong with himself, when he came in contact with others. He found it hard, at times, to live in fellowship with his brethren, not because there may have been faults in them, but because there were faults in him. So this caused him to think and to seek to correct his ways, and in that way it was an on-going salvation.

Then we saw that the most important gathering of the Christians, for this particular day-to-day salvation, was not the Bible Study, as one might imagine; nor was it the Prayer Meeting, but strange to say, it was the Breaking of Bread service. This was the meeting that God had ordained to be the prominent facet in our day-to-day salvation. Now that also was on the first day of the week, strangely enough.

THE GRACE OF GIVING

How to Give

Now, we find that something else happens on the first day of the week. Not only was the coming of the Spirit, in Acts, chapter 2, to baptise the believers, on the first day of the week; not only was the gathering together to break bread, on the first day of the week; but here is another thing that was on the first day of the week - the setting aside of our finances.

Now, this is a difficult subject for many of the speakers because, well, it is embarrassing. However, I want to speak perfectly freely and to show you some of the beautiful features connected with this lovely thing, this giving of our substance.

Firstly, I would like you to notice, particularly, what I read in verse 7, of chapter 8, of II Corinthians, "Therefore, as ye abound in every thing". Oh what a lovely thing! For an Assembly to abound in faith, and to abound in utterance, and to abound in knowledge, and to abound in diligence, and to abound in love, but there is one other thing that the Lord would desire of the Assembly: That it would abound in its Giving.

God has put Giving along with faith! There are some of us

Church Principles for Today

and, perhaps, we are not recognised for our faith, we are a little like Thomas. (There are one, or two, men in the New Testament Scriptures, who have been a tremendous encouragement to me and one of them was Thomas, another was Mark and another was Peter. Those three men mean the world to me because I am like all three of them). It would be a wonderful thing to abound in faith, but God says, 'I want you to abound also in Giving.' And actually, He equates the Gift of Faith with the Grace of Giving. Imagine!

Then He says, 'Utterance and knowledge'. What a lovely thing it would be to have knowledge. One day, the king said to old Galilio, 'You know, sir, I would give all the world to have your knowledge'. To which Galilo answered, 'That is exactly what it cost me'. There is only one way to gain knowledge - get down and study! We saw that in chapter 4. Would it not be a wonderful thing to abound in knowledge? The Lord said, 'Yes, it is a wonderful thing, indeed, but I would like to equate it to with the grace of Giving'.

While it might be that some of the beloved saints cannot abound in faith, and cannot abound in knowledge, then here is a way that they can abound. They can abound in Giving.

THE GRACE OF GIVING

Now it is an interesting thing, that in the Gospel according to Mark, chapter 12, and verse 41, the Lord Jesus sat by the treasury and He watched 'how' they put into the box. I have often thought that the Lord has not changed since then: He still watches, diligently, 'how' we put into the box. I will explain what I mean by, 'the box' in a moment. It does not say that the Lord sat by the treasury to see 'how much' they put into the box. Now I want you to notice that particularly: Not, 'how much', but rather, 'how' the people cast money into the treasury.

This, 'how', is what I want to get at, because it is that which means so much to God, while the, 'how much' is of little importance to Him. 'For the cattle ... not on a thousand hills ... but the cattle on ten thousand hills are His', and the Lord could supply every need on this Earth without one of us. He has His ways of doing everything.

The Lord Jesus is not so much interested in what we give but He is interested in, 'how' we give. What I want to do is to explain this to you from taking this Old Testament Scripture and then bringing it into the New, and to see that every feature in this Feast of Firstfruits, in the Old Testament, is mirrored by similar things in II Corinthians, chapters 8 and 9.

'How' shall I give? One of the very first things that we learn about the Feast of Firstfruits is that it was a very simple feast. These Children of Israel were walking through a waste, barren, desert-land and eventually came to the land of Canaan, where the soil was fertile. The seed they had carried from the land of Egypt, in their little bags, and cared for those forty years, they sowed into the ground and it began to grow. The very first thing that they did, at harvest-time, was to take the first sheaf and offer it to God.

Now, why were they able to do that? They were able to pray at the end of those forty years, 'Lord, You watched over us when we came from Egypt, You watched over us every step of the way. You kept us from this thing and You kept us from that, and You kept us from the disease. Ten thousand fell at our right hand, but it did not come our way and we took it from You, as we travelled through the waste, howling wilderness. You brought us through the Jordan and here we are. This is where Thou hast brought us. Take this, Lord, in appreciation for all Thy kindness.' I am going to write over that, that they gave, 'thankfully'.

THE GRACE OF GIVING

These are days, when many people's pockets are full of money. Can you look back to a time, in your life, when you did not have so much? Can you look back to the time when you neither had in you, or on you? Some can. Yet today finds us with homes, and carpets, and cars, and clothes, and more than we need. Tell me, where do you get it?

"I worked for it. I studied for it. I slaved for it."

"Did you?"

The Lord could have snapped His fingers at your health, when you were a little child, and made you permanently ill! The Epistle of James says, 'Everything you have, you got from God'.

Where is your thanks? What God is bringing before me, in this lovely scene, is that when, 'Thou comest into the land, do not forget, sir, and give Me the firstfruits of your increase.' He does not say, 'Will you?' He says, 'Do it'.

When we come to II Corinthians, chapter 9, verse 8, it says, "And God is able to make all grace abound toward you", and that is what He has done with me for years. He has made His grace abound. Super-abound! Overwhelmingly abound! So that, sometimes, when my wife and I are talking on these things, we marvel at what God has done. Did you ever do that? Well, after you have done that, would you like to show Him a little appreciation and give Him something back? How shall I give? You shall give, 'thankfully'.

How shall I give? There is an offering known as the Burnt Offering and while I am not going to go into the details of it, lovely as that study would be, there is one word that we could write over it, and that is, 'love', or dedication: An expression of my love.

It was my little grand child's birthday, recently, and I wanted to show her how much I loved her but, you have to be careful what you buy a little child now-a-days. Most little children have a bicycle but hers was bought when she was very young and she had grown too big for it. So, in order to show my love, I bought her a brand new bicycle.

Would you like to show your love to God? You are not only thankful for what He has done for you, but you want to show Him that you love Him. The Lord Jesus would sit by the treas-

THE GRACE OF GIVING

ury and watch how you put in. He sees if you put in, 'lovingly'.

This is what we have in II Corinthians, chapter 8, verse 5, where it reads, "And this they did, not as we had hoped, but first gave their own selves to the Lord". Further, it says in chapter 12, verse 1, of the Roman Epistle, "I beseech you therefore, brethren, by the mercies of God, that ye present your bodies a living sacrifice ... unto God". The Lord Jesus wants to know how I give. He wants me to give thankfully, and lovingly.

If I loved the Lord, with all my heart, it would not be hard for Him to get something out of my pocket! You show me somebody that I love and I will show you somebody that has not much trouble to get a few pence from me. You know that is true!

In the Old Testament, one had to present a Meal Offering. I am not going to go into the details of that offering, beautiful as that might be, but there is one word that I can write over it and that is the word, sincerity. The man gave sincerely. Do you give, 'sincerely', or hypocritically?

Church Principles for Today

I used to know a man, and I knew for a fact, that this man's wife and little children had nothing to eat at home. That dear man, and he was a dear man in a thousand different ways, was seen to put pound notes onto the collection plate - while his wife had neither in her, nor on her. That was down right hypocrisy!

My God demands that you look after your wife and little family, and if you do not, you are worse than an infidel. So, when you give, He wants you to give with a sincere heart.

Notice what it says in II Corinthians, chapter 8, verses 8 and 9, "I speak not by commandment, but by occasion of the forwardness of others, and to prove the sincerity of your love. For you know the grace of our Lord Jesus Christ, that, though He was rich, yet for your sakes He became poor". How shall I give? I shall give it, 'thankfully', I shall give it, 'lovingly', I shall give it, 'sincerely'.

In Old Testament times when one offered these firstfruits, one had also to present a Drink Offering. I am not going to go into the details of the Drink Offering, but the saints who have studied that offering will know that you could write one word

THE GRACE OF GIVING

over it, and that is, 'joy'. They gave it, 'joyfully'.

What a lovely thing to put your hand in your pocket, at the end of the week, or at the beginning of the week (it does not matter as we will see) and to give unto the Lord with a happy, happy heart. Cheerfully, if you like.

In II Corinthians, chapter 9, verse 7, it says, "Every man according as he purposeth in his heart, so let him give; not grudgingly, or of necessity: for God loveth a cheerful giver" - or better, hilarious giver! He wants us to give, 'cheerfully'.

As the Lord sits by the treasury and watches me, watches you, week-by-week; does He see us taking of our substance and giving it to Him willingly, thankfully, lovingly, sincerely and cheerfully?

Then, there was another offering and this is the one that goes to the very core of my soul. In those Firstfruits, in Leviticus, chapter 23, the man put that first sheaf of corn in his hand, the very best that he could get and he moved it, backwards and forwards, before the God of Heaven. He did that because, it was

Church Principles for Today

called a Wave Offering. If we were to study that offering, I think that you would be able to agree with me that the wave offering could be covered by one word, and that is, 'scrutiny'.

Now this may be a sore point, but if you have earned your money dishonestly, then the Lord just does not want it! You can keep it! He does not watch whether you give Him £100, or only £1, but do not forget before you give it, to wave it. Whenever you have something in your heart to give, and you are going to give thankfully, lovingly, sincerely, cheerfully, but make sure you got it. 'honestly'. Make sure you can put that £100, or £1, in the palm of your hand, literally, if you feel that way inclined, and wave it before the God of Heaven. If you can say, 'With my hands I earned this money, honestly, before the sight of God and men,' then give it, but if you cannot say that, put it in your pocket again, for God does not want it. He would rather see five pence in the box, that was honestly earned, than ten thousand pounds that was got by roguery, or trickery. Just you wave it before God and then give it to Him. If you cannot wave it, then keep it and spend it on something else!

Oh, I tell you, this has exercised my heart. This has gone down to the depths of my soul for years, and burned into my

THE GRACE OF GIVING

conscience. That £1 I give to God, have I earned it honestly?

Listen to what it says in the passage which we read, (II Corinthians, chapter 8, verse 21) "Providing for honest things, not only in the sight of the Lord, but also in the sight of men."

What a lovely thing, for those who take charge of the finances of the Church to be able to say that also! Of course, the brethren will know that I am not seeking to reproach them, I would not do a thing like that, but that is the way the finances of the Assembly should be run, too. We know that the brethren are not rogues. We know that what they do, they do honestly. But remember that God commands everything to be done correctly, not only in the sight of God, but also in the sight of men. God demands that we should not only do things right but that they are seen to be done right.

I remember, one time, being at an Assembly Annual Meeting, and a brother gave an announcement of all the money and how it had been spent. After giving his report of the accounts, he put the books beside him, on the bench, and said, "These books are for the scrutiny of every member of the Assembly who wants to look at them." I thought, that was a lovely gesture! Honest, not only in the sight of the Lord, but also in the sight of men. Thus saith the Holy Scripture.

Matthew, chapter 5, verses 23 and 24 says, "Therefore if thou bring thy gift to the altar ..." (So, here I am coming with my money), "and there rememberest that thy brother hath ought against thee"; just leave your gift there, sir. Just leave it where it is. Go, and first be reconciled with thy brother, and then come and offer thy gift. God does not want money from you that is not gained by honest means.

If the Lord has some missionary, or evangelist, or some needy saint to take care of, He will take care of them from some other source. He does not want any ill-gotten gains.

We also notice, in II Corinthians, that the Lord not only wants you to give thankfully, lovingly, sincerely, cheerfully and honourably, but He wants you to give, 'liberally'.

At last, we are coming to 'how much' we should be giving! When I put my hand in my pocket and give to the Lord my few pence, can I really say, "Lord, I have given You this liberally". Is it a liberal amount? Now, I tell you that will search the heart.

THE GRACE OF GIVING

This is not a matter of waiting until Sunday morning and putting my hand in my pocket to find how much I have and putting that into the collection, then, forgetting the whole thing. Do you think that is liberal? When some are earning £400 a week, or more, would you look on that spare £0.50 as being liberal? I do not think that I would.

Not so very long ago I was speaking to a young saint who was very interested in how much she should give to the Lord. She said, "I have not got very much." All I said to her was, "Well, how has the Lord prospered you, dear? Give accordingly as to how the Lord has prospered you? Give it thankfully, lovingly, sincerely, cheerfully, honourably and whatever you give, make it as liberally as you can."

I Corinthians, chapter 16, verse 2, reads like this, "Upon the first day of the week let every one of you lay by him in store, as God hath prospered him." That, to me, simply means, 'systematically'. God does not want me to be a haphazard giver, He wants me to do things with a mind, and a heart, that works. He wants me to put figures to the test. He wants me to give it according to a systematic base. This is what I get as a wage – now, how much can I give? Systematically.

Church Principles for Today

I was across in England some time ago, and was staying in a dear brother's home. He is out in full-time service. It is not often these beloved brethren say much about their finances. But this brother, because he had known me for many years, and I was a very dear friend of his, as he is of mine, let me into one little secret. He said,

"Rowan, I want to tell you something. You know those two saints who lived on the other side of the city?"

I said, "I know them well."

He said, "I want to tell you something about them. From the very day that I went out in full-time service, to this very day, their cheque has arrived on the first day of every month".

What do you think of that for systematic giving? It put me to downright shame. Now, he did not say whether it was much, or little. It might have been only for a pound, but the one thing that thrilled his soul, was that from the day that he went out in full-time service, to this day, he could look forward, and with dependency, to the first day of every month, to get a little amount from them. Systematically.

This shows me, perfectly clearly, that it does not matter

THE GRACE OF GIVING

whether I give on the first day of the week, or the last day of the week, just as long as I give.

There is another way in which we must give and that is, 'sympathetically'. I want you to consider this very carefully. I do not find much trouble in deciding how much I have to give the Lord. I keep books. I keep a budget. I know exactly what I earn. I know exactly what I have to do with it. I have no problem. When I weigh up my books at the end of the year I know exactly where I stand, almost to the last penny. I work it all out. It is not hard for me to decide what is liberal to the Lord. But I will tell you where my problem comes. What am I going to do with it? Now, there is a problem. What are you going to do with it, now that you have it? That is what I mean by sympathetic giving.

With all due respects to the collection in the Assembly, I want you to remember that you must also be a sympathetic giver. Remember, there are other things that need to be attended to, as well as the Assembly. I Corinthians, chapter 16, tells me that there are needy saints. If I know of a needy saint, I am not going to go and tell you. Do you think I will tell you if I know of a dear soul that is hungry? No, I would not! I would look after him myself. That means that I cannot put all that I lay aside into the collection box. It is an exercise between you, the saint, and the Lord. That is what I mean by sympathetic giving.

Listen to I Timothy, chapter 5: 'Do not forget the widow,' says the apostle. There are some widows that do not have very much. In the newspapers, every day, we read about poor souls that are living all alone, who do not know when they are going to get their next meal, and cannot pay their winter's electric bills. Why? Because they cannot live on their widow's pension! Do you know any of those dear souls? There are plenty of them. Do not forget them. Call and see them every-so-often, and bring them a little something to cheer their poor hearts. Sympathetic. It does not all go into the box.

What about the elders? Oh, they do not need any money! The elders have always plenty. In I Timothy, chapter 5, I find that there is a certain type of elder, who never ceases to visit the flock, and he never goes without bringing something with him. Do you know what I mean? Where do you think he is getting the money from? Perhaps you have no time for such things. Well, if you were an elder and had been visiting the sick, and elderly, for years, and maybe you are, yourself, on the pension,

THE GRACE OF GIVING

where are you going to get the money to bring the sick those oranges, and apples, and a little cake? 'Well'? Says the Lord, 'Look after the elders that do this sort of thing and make sure you give sympathetically'. To an elder? Yes. I am not thinking about myself for I am not an old age pensioner. However, in another six years I will be – then you can consider it!

I Corinthians, chapter 9, mentions the evangelist. What about him? We give to evangelists through the collection boxes. Oh, I know you do and that is lovely, but I want to tell you that there are some evangelists and the brethren know nothing about them. I could tell you about a lot of evangelists in England, Scotland and Wales and they are never heard of. I know some of them could use a couple of pounds. Some of them have not the means hardly to clothe themselves and their little families.

I remember, not so very long ago, we had a brother in our home and do you know what he told me (because some of these dear brethren get to trust you, although they usually tell little, if anything). He said, "Rowan, I have not got enough money to pay the electricity bill and I received a letter the other day. We are in debt." What do you think of that? Now, if the saints had been doing, what they should have been doing he would not have been like that. These men are out in full-time service, they are preaching the Gospel of the Lord Jesus Christ. Do not forget them. Give sympathetically, to the needy saints, to the widows, to the elders, to the evangelists.

What about the teachers? Galatians, chapter 6, and verse 6, talks about them. 'Do not forget them', it says. And verse 10 says, 'do not forget all men'. There are people, out there, who are not saved and know nothing about God, but do not forget them. So, while I must look after the Assembly and make sure I pay for the electricity, the cleaner, the taxes and the insurance, I must also make sure that I do not forget that there are needy saints, and widows, and elders, and evangelists, and teachers, and all men, who have to be cared for. Sympathetic giving. Consider all the channels.

So here, Lord, I have set aside liberally. Look, I have gained it honestly. I am giving it back to Thee, cheerfully, lovingly, thankfully, and all the rest, but I am going to keep some back for this soul, and a little for that purpose. I am going to give sympathetically. See Figure 9.1:

THE GRACE OF GIVING

Rewards for Giving

Will I get a reward for giving? Indeed you will, for giving is well-pleasing to God. Philippians, chapter 4, verse 8 and Hebrews, chapter 13, verse 16, says that when the Lord looks down, from Heaven, and sees me laying aside my little portion, it rises up to His nostrils as a smell of a sweet fragrance. It gives the Lord great delight and pleasure, when I set aside my money. Surely, that is reward enough!

Says II Corinthians, 'It brings thanks to God'. If you were in need and a knock came at the door and someone handed in a couple of pounds to buy the things you need, do you know the very first thing you would do? You would get down on your knees and give God thanks. The result of their giving, therefore, is that thanks are given to God. Surely that is another reward, that the One you love, is given pleasure, and appreciated, because of your giving.

There are dozens of other rewards too. But may God grant, indeed, that we might know what it is to give thankfully, lovingly, sincerely, joyfully, honestly liberally, systematically, and also sympathetically.

Appendix

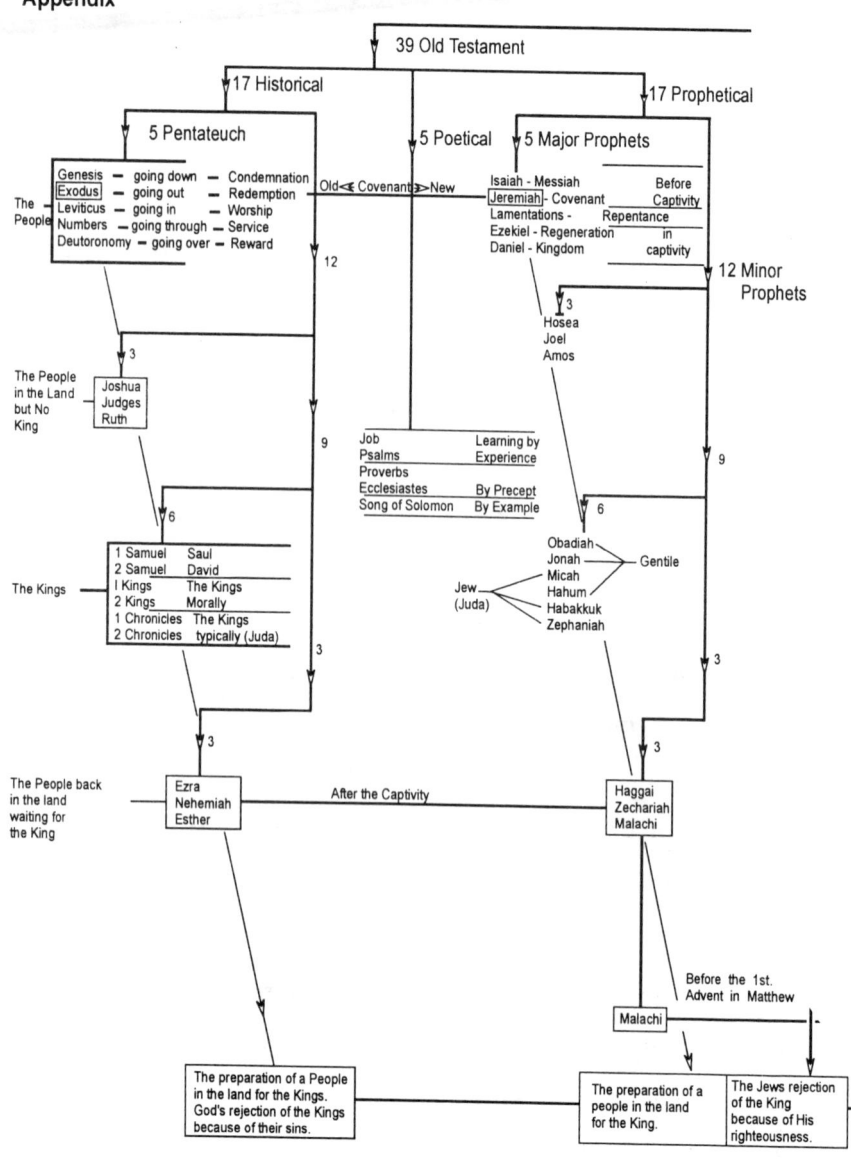

39 Old Testament

17 Historical

5 Pentateuch

The People:
- Genesis — going down — Condemnation
- Exodus — going out — Redemption
- Leviticus — going in — Worship
- Numbers — going through — Service
- Deuteronomy — going over — Reward

Old ← Covenant → New

The People in the Land but No King (3):
- Joshua
- Judges
- Ruth

The Kings (6):
- 1 Samuel — Saul
- 2 Samuel — David
- 1 Kings — The Kings
- 2 Kings — Morally
- 1 Chronicles — The Kings
- 2 Chronicles — typically (Juda)

The People back in the land waiting for the King (3):
- Ezra
- Nehemiah
- Esther

After the Captivity

5 Poetical

- Job — Learning by Experience
- Psalms
- Proverbs
- Ecclesiastes — By Precept
- Song of Solomon — By Example

17 Prophetical

5 Major Prophets

- Isaiah - Messiah — Before Captivity
- Jeremiah - Covenant — Repentance
- Lamentations - Repentance — in captivity
- Ezekiel - Regeneration
- Daniel - Kingdom

12 Minor Prophets

(3):
- Hosea
- Joel
- Amos

(6):
- Obadiah
- Jonah → Gentile
- Micah
- Hahum
- Habakkuk
- Zephaniah

Jew (Juda)

(3):
- Haggai
- Zechariah
- Malachi

Before the 1st. Advent in Matthew

Malachi

- The preparation of a People in the land for the Kings. God's rejection of the Kings because of their sins.
- The preparation of a people in the land for the King.
- The Jews rejection of the King because of His righteousness.

AN OUTLINE OF THE RELATIONSHIP

66 Books Whole Bible

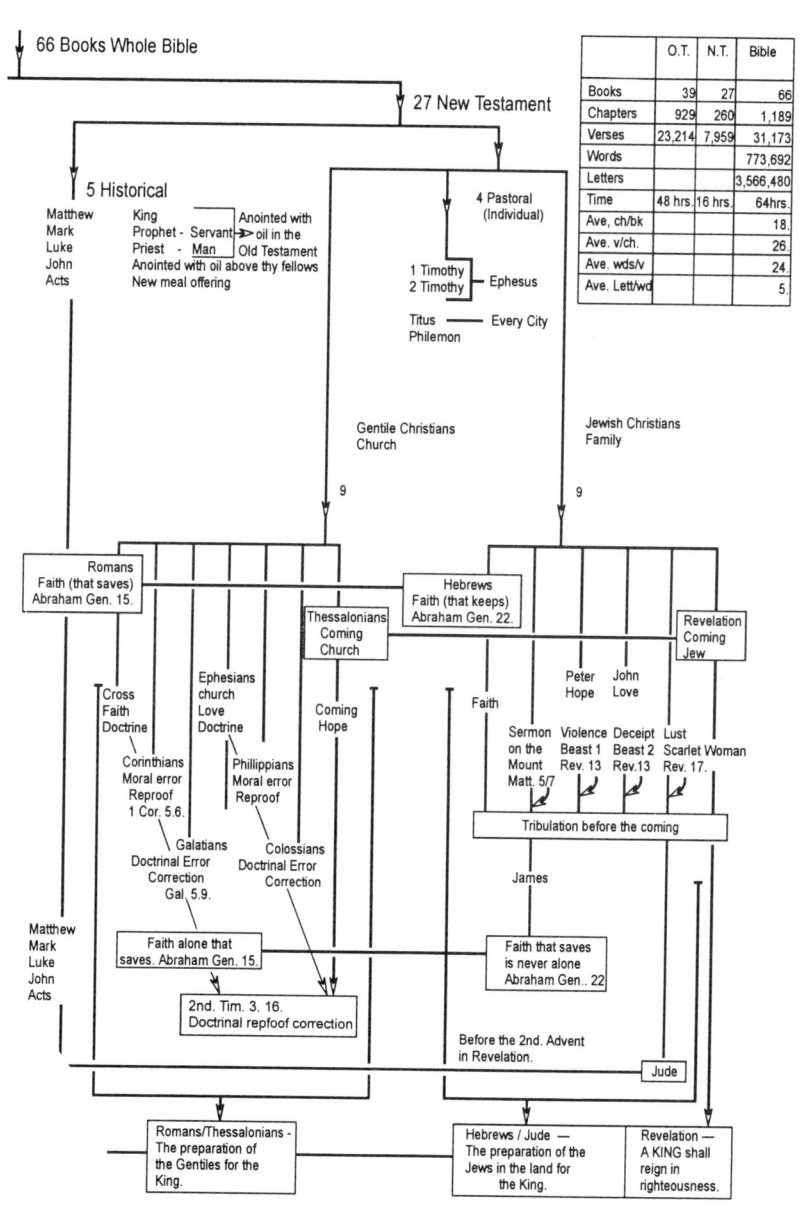

	O.T.	N.T.	Bible
Books	39	27	66
Chapters	929	260	1,189
Verses	23,214	7,959	31,173
Words			773,692
Letters			3,566,480
Time	48 hrs.	16 hrs.	64hrs.
Ave. ch/bk			18
Ave. v/ch.			26
Ave. wds/v			24
Ave. Lett/wd			5

27 New Testament

5 Historical
Matthew
Mark
Luke
John
Acts

King — Anointed with
Prophet - Servant → oil in the
Priest - Man — Old Testament
Anointed with oil above thy fellows
New meal offering

4 Pastoral (Individual)

1 Timothy ⎫
2 Timothy ⎬ Ephesus

Titus ⎫
Philemon ⎬ Every City

Gentile Christians — Church

Jewish Christians — Family

9 / 9

Romans — Faith (that saves) Abraham Gen. 15.

Hebrews — Faith (that keeps) Abraham Gen. 22.

Thessalonians Coming Church

Revelation Coming Jew

Cross / Faith / Doctrine

Ephesians — church Love Doctrine

Coming Hope

Faith

Peter — Hope
John — Love

Corinthians Moral error Reproof 1 Cor. 5.6.

Phillippians Moral error Reproof

Sermon on the Mount Matt. 5/7

Violence Beast 1 Rev. 13

Deceipt Beast 2 Rev.13

Lust Scarlet Woman Rev. 17.

Galatians Doctrinal Error Correction Gal. 5.9.

Colossians Doctrinal Error Correction

Tribulation before the coming

James

Matthew
Mark
Luke
John
Acts

Faith alone that saves. Abraham Gen. 15.

Faith that saves is never alone Abraham Gen.. 22

2nd. Tim. 3. 16. Doctrinal reproof correction

Before the 2nd. Advent in Revelation.

Jude

| Romans/Thessalonians - The preparation of the Gentiles for the King. | Hebrews / Jude — The preparation of the Jews in the land for the King. | Revelation — A KING shall reign in righteousness. |

OF THE BOOKS OF THE **BIBLE**.

R. Jennings

INDEX

Index

Genesis
- 3   Pg.295, Pg.310,
- 6   Pg.303,
- 15   Pg.31,
- 22   Pg.31,

Exodus
- 20   Pg.227,
- 20:15 Pg.268,

Leviticus
- 23   Pg.329,
- 23:9 Pg.316,
- 24   Pg.152,

Numbers
- 15   Pg.153,

Joshua
- 20   Pg.90, Pg.90,
- 20:1 Pg.47,

Psalm
- 2:6   Pg.238,
- 2:9   Pg.237,
- 22   Pg.123,
- 22:14 Pg.248,

Proverbs
- 22:6 Pg.271,

Isaiah
- 50:6 Pg.248,

Matthew
- 3   Pg.112,
- 3:11 Pg.116,
- 5:23 Pg.332,
- 8   Pg.165,
- 11:28 Pg.193,
- 16   Pg.58,
- 18   Pg.285,
- 25:21 Pg.43,
- 26:27 Pg.231,

Mark
- 1   Pg.112,
- 12:41 Pg.323,
- 14:23 Pg.231,

Luke
- 1   Pg.117,
- 3   Pg.112,
- 6:46 Pg.245,
- 7   Pg.170,
- 22:20 Pg.232,
- 23   Pg.230,

John
- 1   Pg.112,
- 3:16 Pg.193,
- 3:36 Pg.193,
- 4   Pg.120,
- 5:22 Pg.265,
- 5:24 Pg.193,
- 10   Pg.71,

Acts
- 1   Pg.55,
- 2   Pg.55, Pg.74, Pg.119, Pg.120, Pg.126, Pg.157, Pg.188, Pg.319, Pg.321,
- 2:2-4 Pg.119,
- 8   Pg.121, Pg.127,
- 9   Pg.186,
- 10   Pg.122, Pg.157, Pg.186,
- 11   Pg.112,
- 13   Pg.14,
- 13:2-14:27 Pg.17,
- 15:36-18:22 Pg.17,
- 18:23-21:17 Pg.17,
- 19   Pg.124, Pg.158,
- 20   Pg.84,
- 26:31-28:16 Pg.17,
- 28:30 Pg.15,

Romans
- 1-5:11 Pg.41,
- 8:31 Pg.41,
- 5   Pg.39,
- 5:12-7:6 Pg.41,

343

6	Pg.165, Pg.189, Pg.194, Pg.210, Pg.211, Pg.212, Pg.213, Pg.214, Pg.215,		Pg.199, Pg.210, Pg.215, Pg.246,
6:1-9	Pg.182,	10:1-4	Pg.181,
7:6	Pg.39,	10:11	Pg.182,
7:7-8:30	Pg.41,	11	Pg.185, Pg.219, Pg.296, Pg.302, Pg.309, Pg.221, Pg.235, Pg.241, Pg.242, Pg.243, Pg.246, Pg.249, Pg.294,
8	Pg.159, Pg.49, Pg.132,		
8:1	Pg.103,		
8:9	Pg.128,	11:2-	Pg.291,
8:31	Pg.36,	11:11	Pg.304,
8:33	Pg.12,	11:16	Pg.307,
8:35	Pg.40,	11:23-	Pg.217,
9	Pg.41,	11:25	Pg.232,
9:1-11:32	Pg.41,	11:26	Pg.224,
10:9	Pg.230,	11:27	Pg.235,
11:33	Pg.12,	11:28	Pg.241,
12	Pg.42,	11:29	Pg.235,
12:1	Pg.327,	11:32	Pg.235,
13	Pg.42,	12	Pg.82, Pg.112, Pg.118, Pg.128, Pg.151, Pg.190,
13:1	Pg.265,		
14	Pg.42,	12:12-	Pg.83,
15	Pg.42,	12:13	Pg.128,
16	Pg.42,	14	Pg.172, Pg.172, Pg.175, Pg.294, Pg.296,
16:25-27	Pg.43,		
		14:2	Pg.159,
		14:20-	Pg.147,

I Corinthians

		14:33-	Pg.292,
3	Pg.85, Pg.85, Pg.102, Pg.144,	16	Pg.335,
		16:2	Pg.333,
3:6	Pg.144,	22:24	Pg.248,
3:17	Pg.255,	**II Corinthians**	
5	Pg.31, Pg.32, Pg.103, Pg.281, Pg.281,	2,7	Pg.281,
		8 & 9	Pg.324,
5:1	Pg.253,	8:1-24	Pg.317,
5:6	Pg.277,	8:8-9	Pg.328,
5:11	Pg.283,	8:9	Pg.327,
6	Pg.59,	9:7	Pg.329,
8:7	Pg.321,	9:8	Pg.325,
8:21	Pg.331,	10	Pg.187,
9	Pg.337,	11	Pg.88,
10	Pg.199, Pg.189, Pg.190, Pg.194, Pg.195, Pg.197,	**Galatians**	
		5	Pg.31,

6:6   Pg.338,
Ephesians
1   Pg.59,
1:20-   Pg.109,
1:22   Pg.61,
1:25-   Pg.46,
2   Pg.62,
2:6-8   Pg.110,
3   Pg.63,Pg.155,
3:1   Pg.18,
3:9-   Pg.110,
4   Pg.64, Pg.151, Pg.18,
4:11-   Pg.110,
5   Pg.62,Pg.134,
5:25-   Pg.46,
6:20   Pg.18,
Philippians
1:7, 13, 14, 16
        Pg.19,
1:19   Pg.19,
2   Pg.304,
3   Pg.123,
4   Pg.278,
4:8   Pg.339,
Colossians
1:24   Pg.19,
4:3, 18 Pg.19,
4:10   Pg.19,
I Thessalonians
4   Pg.55,
I Timothy
2   Pg.294,
2:8-   Pg.293,
3   Pg.87,
5   Pg.289,Pg.336,
II Timothy
3   Pg.175,
4:6, 7 Pg.20,
Titus
1   Pg.287,
1:9   Pg.286,
2   Pg.312,
3   Pg.283,

3:9-14 Pg.284,
Philemon
1   Pg.19,
10, 13 Pg.19,
23   Pg.19,
Hebrews
2   Pg.59,
3   Pg.73,
4   Pg.94,
6   Pg.209,
8 & 10 Pg.102,
8:10   Pg.249,
10   Pg.227,
12   Pg.74,Pg.246, Pg.268, Pg.270,
13:16   Pg.339,
I Peter
3   Pg.187,Pg.189,Pg.194, Pg.204, Pg.206, Pg.210, Pg.215,
3:15-   Pg.183,
5   Pg.84,
Pg.106,
I John
5:12   Pg.193,
Revelation
1   Pg.88,Pg.136,Pg.137,
1:18-   Pg.111,
1:19-   Pg.46,
2,3   Pg.23,
3   Pg.107,
21   Pg.73,